Schmelvis

In Search of Elvis Presley's Jewish Roots

Schmelvis

JONATHAN GOLDSTEIN & MAX WALLACE

ECW PRESS

Published by ECW Press
2120 Queen Street East, Suite 200, Toronto, Ontario, Canada M4E 1E2

NATIONAL LIBRARY OF CANADA CATALOGUING IN PUBLICATION DATA

Goldstein, Jonathan, 1969-
Schmelvis: in search of Elvis Presley's Jewish roots
ISBN 1-55022-462-X
Presley, Elvis, 1935-1977—Humor I. Wallace, Max II. Title.
ML420.P74G624 2002   782.42166'092   C2001-900539-

Interior and back cover photos and stills: Mila Aung Thwin and Max Wallace
Editor: Francesca LoDico
Cover design: Guylaine Régimbald—Solo Design
Design layout and typesetting: Guylaine Régimbald—Solo Design
Production: Heather Bean
Printing: Transcontinental

This book is set in Utopia, Letter Gothic, Briem Akademi, Arial, and Allise

The publication of *Schmelvis: In Search of Elvis Presley's Jewish Roots* has been generously supported by the Canada Council, the Ontario Arts Council, and the Government of Canada through the Book Industry Development Program. Canadä

Distribution

CANADA
General Distribution Services, 325 Humber College Blvd., Toronto, ON M9W 7C3

UNITED STATES
Independent Publishers Group, 814 North Franklin Street, Chicago, Illinois 60610

EUROPE
Turnaround Publisher Services, Unit 3, Olympia Trading Estate, Coburg Road, Wood Green, London N2Z 6T2

AUSTRALIA AND NEW ZEALAND
Wakefield Press, 17 Rundle Street (Box 2066), Kent Town, South Australia 5071

ECW PRESS   ecwpress.com

Jon's Dedication

For my Aunt Tillie, the first person to ever make me really, really laugh.

I would like to express my gratitude to the cast and crew for being such fun travel mates, Francesca LoDico for her editorial acumen, and my parents for instilling in me a real love of Elvis. I would especially like to extend a pinky in thanks to my friend Evan Beloff, who was of immeasurable service during this book's writing.

Max's Dedication

To the King, whose spirit guided this whole *meshuggah* enterprise.

I don't know whether thanks is the appropriate acknowledgment for my esteemed colleagues Evan Beloff and Ari Cohen, without whom I would still have a modicum of dignity left. But in between the craziness, it's been fun. And I'd also like to thank Francesca LoDico, Guylaine Régimbald, and Heather Bean of ECW for helping to turn a strange film into an even stranger book.

To view footage from the film "*Schmelvis: Searching For the King's Jewish Roots*," go to www.schmelvis.com.

Schmelvis: In Search of Elvis Presley's Jewish Roots is loosely based on the documentary produced by Diversus Productions. Many of the scenes are satirical recreations of the way the authors remember the making of the documentary. However, all the facts pertaining to Elvis's actual Jewish roots are authentic.

Table of Contents

Part 1

All Shook Up in the Holy Land: Pilgrims Honor Elvis's Yahrzeit

By Joshua Harris Prager
Staff Reporter of THE WALL STREET JOURNAL

Hundreds of Israelis trekked to a wooded spot southwest of Jerusalem yesterday to commemorate the King's death. Not the biblical monarch David, but Elvis Presley.

Biannually, Elvis enthusiasts in Israel gather at the Elvis Inn, a restaurant and gas station in the Neveh Ilan area that moonlights as a shrine to the late rocker. It isn't your average Elvis sanctuary.

Some of the Elvis impersonators wear not only rhinestone-spangled white jumpsuits but also yarmulkes. Scads of flickering yahrzeit candles, lit according to Jewish mourning ritual, memorialize Mr. Presley. Draped around the neck of a 13-foot brass statue of Mr. Presley is a pendant reading *chai*, the Hebrew word for alive and a Jewish talisman.

"When people ask why I put a chai on him, I show them the picture of Elvis performing in Salt Lake City," says Uri Yoeli, the inn's owner. "Then they know."

Sure enough, the photograph taken in the early 1970s shows the King wearing a chai. The picture, says Mr. Yoeli, 51, is testament to Mr. Presley's Jewish roots. "Elvis's middle name was Aharon!" exults Mr. Yoeli, using the Hebrew for Aaron. Elvis spelled it Aron.

According to "Elvis and Gladys," a 1985 book by Elaine Dundy, Elvis's maternal great-great-grandmother Nancy Tackett was Jewish. Her daughter Martha Tackett gave birth to Doll Mansell who gave birth to Gladys Smith who gave birth to Elvis. So, according to Jewish law which stipulates that Jewish identity is passed on matrilineally, Mr. Presley was Jewish.

"We know there is Jewish heritage in Elvis's family going a few generations back," confirms Todd Morgan, a spokesman at Graceland, the Memphis, Tenn., museum and former Presley home. "It was something Elvis was aware of and certainly was sensitive to."

Though Elvis wasn't raised Jewish, he was familiar with Jewish customs from a young age. As a teenager, Elvis and his family rented the bottom apartment of a duplex in Memphis. Rabbi Alfred and Jeannette Fruchter lived upstairs and were Orthodox Jews. "On the [Jewish] Sabbath you're not supposed to turn on lights," Mr. Morgan explains. "Elvis would go in and do that for this family."

Mr. Presley remained in touch with his Jewish heritage. When his mother died, he made sure to have a Jewish star put on her headstone. "In essence he was a devout man," Mr. Yoeli says. "He believed in God."

Evan

Ari

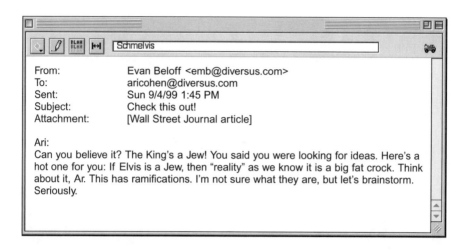

From: Evan Beloff <emb@diversus.com>
To: aricohen@diversus.com
Sent: Sun 9/4/99 1:45 PM
Subject: Check this out!
Attachment: [Wall Street Journal article]

Ari:
Can you believe it? The King's a Jew! You said you were looking for ideas. Here's a hot one for you: If Elvis is a Jew, then "reality" as we know it is a big fat crock. Think about it, Ar. This has ramifications. I'm not sure what they are, but let's brainstorm. Seriously.

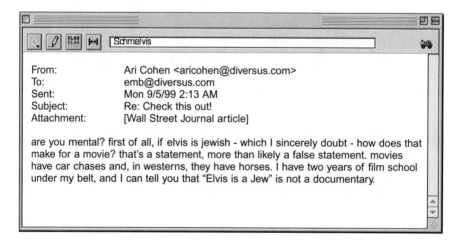

From: Ari Cohen <aricohen@diversus.com>
To: emb@diversus.com
Sent: Mon 9/5/99 2:13 AM
Subject: Re: Check this out!
Attachment: [Wall Street Journal article]

are you mental? first of all, if elvis is jewish - which I sincerely doubt - how does that make for a movie? that's a statement, more than likely a false statement. movies have car chases and, in westerns, they have horses. I have two years of film school under my belt, and I can tell you that "Elvis is a Jew" is not a documentary.

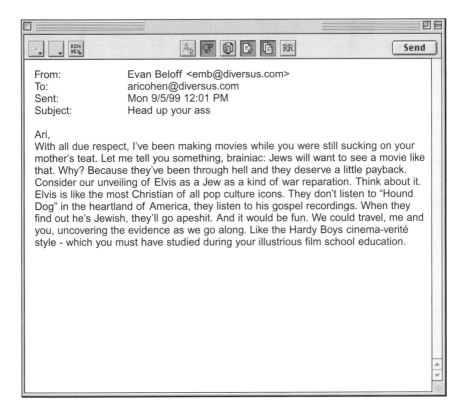

From: Evan Beloff <emb@diversus.com>
To: aricohen@diversus.com
Sent: Mon 9/5/99 12:01 PM
Subject: Head up your ass

Ari,
With all due respect, I've been making movies while you were still sucking on your mother's teat. Let me tell you something, brainiac: Jews will want to see a movie like that. Why? Because they've been through hell and they deserve a little payback. Consider our unveiling of Elvis as a Jew as a kind of war reparation. Think about it. Elvis is like the most Christian of all pop culture icons. They don't listen to "Hound Dog" in the heartland of America, they listen to his gospel recordings. When they find out he's Jewish, they'll go apeshit. And it would be fun. We could travel, me and you, uncovering the evidence as we go along. Like the Hardy Boys cinema-verité style - which you must have studied during your illustrious film school education.

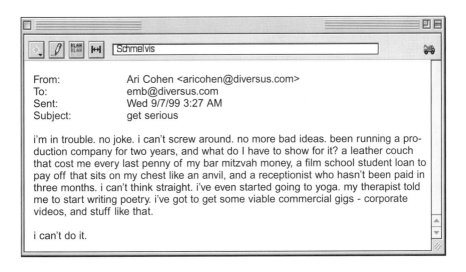

From: Ari Cohen <aricohen@diversus.com>
To: emb@diversus.com
Sent: Wed 9/7/99 3:27 AM
Subject: get serious

i'm in trouble. no joke. i can't screw around. no more bad ideas. been running a production company for two years, and what do I have to show for it? a leather couch that cost me every last penny of my bar mitzvah money, a film school student loan to pay off that sits on my chest like an anvil, and a receptionist who hasn't been paid in three months. i can't think straight. i've even started going to yoga. my therapist told me to start writing poetry. i've got to get some viable commercial gigs - corporate videos, and stuff like that.

i can't do it.

19

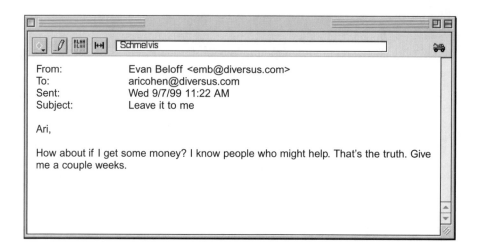

From: Evan Beloff <emb@diversus.com>
To: aricohen@diversus.com
Sent: Wed 9/7/99 11:22 AM
Subject: Leave it to me

Ari,

How about if I get some money? I know people who might help. That's the truth. Give me a couple weeks.

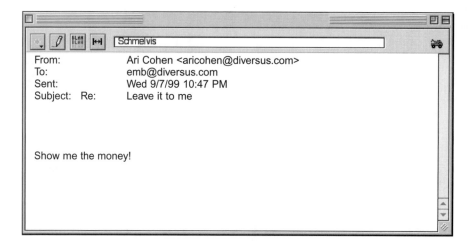

From: Ari Cohen <aricohen@diversus.com>
To: emb@diversus.com
Sent: Wed 9/7/99 10:47 PM
Subject: Re: Leave it to me

Show me the money!

If Elvis is a Jew

If Elvis is a Jew
The wild-eyed ladies of Borneo will rejoice with piña coladas?
The wild grocery-bagged ladies of Brighton Beach will dance can-can down the boardwalk?
The wild-fisted street toughs of Memphis will rabbit punch my uterus?
The wild-haired rabbinical scholars will chant "hound dog" in Aramaic?
If Elvis is a Jew I will walk naked on the bottom of the sea, and bring plastic beads to the shore.

Evan's Production Journal

Just came from Pearlie's. Just a friendly visit. Just to say hi.

Never thought she had any money. She lives in a 1 1/2 near the Decarie Expressway and eats frozen birthday cake. But Neil told me she managed to put away a nest egg from her showbiz days. Ari can try all he wants to get grants, but the only way it's going to happen is with some good old-fashioned pitchmanship.

My Aunt's sharp as a tack, a real find, a trophy. Ninety years old with a shock of flaming red hair. Claims to have had sex with Frank Sinatra. Used to work in the jazz clubs when Montreal was the center of the universe for be-bop in the '30s and '40s. They used to call her Little Pearlie Fields. And her act: Half a pint of the blues and a two-gallon jug of legs.

"I had red hot gams," she'd tell me when I was a kid.

She ran her sports car up a tree once and lived to keep singing.

She hates that I'm a veggie. Every time I go over she tries everything short of cramming a chicken leg down my throat to set me on the path of righteousness.

"What kind of an animal doesn't eat lamb chops?" she asks me, setting down a huge plate of the stuff.

The very smell makes me feel like the walls are closing in.

"You know what they called men like you in the old country, don't you?"

"What's that, Auntie Pearlie?"

"Faggots."

Possible pitches for Pearlie's money

1. Elvis film as legacy ("You're going to die soon and that's life. I could be your heir.")

2. Give Pearlie a role in the film (she's bound to want a little fame in her golden years)

3. The crying plea approach (watch *Duddy Kravitz* again)

4. The angry crying plea approach ("You never loved me. No one loves me. You all want to see me fail.")

5. Film as mitzvah ("You're retrieving a Jewish soul. Do you have any idea what that means? God holds a single Jewish soul to be worth more than all the gems on the earth. You cannot place a value on a Jewish *neshemah*. How dare you place a value on a Jewish *neshemah*?")

6. Sweet-talk her (get drunk enough to feel no pain and take the old yenta dancing)

note: do a lot of dips

THE PITCH

EVAN: We're setting out to prove that Elvis was Jewish.

PEARLIE: Who's Elvis?

EVAN: The King of Rock & Roll. "Hound Dog."

PEARLIE: I know, I know. I thought you said . . . never mind. And how is this going to make money?

EVAN: We've already sold it to a TV station in England.

PEARLIE: Very nice.

EVAN: People are very excited by the project.

PEARLIE: Tell me, you finished school already?

EVAN: I dropped out of school eight years ago, Auntie Pearlie.

PEARLIE: What did you study?

EVAN: Theater.

PEARLIE: Did you know cousin Ruthie's grandson graduated a year ago and now he's a speech therapist?

EVAN: Why are you telling me this?

PEARLIE: I'm just saying. They make a decent wage.

EVAN: I make a decent wage.

PEARLIE: What kind of life is it to not know where your next paycheck is coming from?

EVAN: Auntie Pearlie, I'm very happy with my life.

PEARLIE: Your mother cries herself to sleep over you.

EVAN: Why are you doing this to me?

PEARLIE: When you were a little boy and I used to buy you chocolate bars, you used to nibble at them like a little mouse. I used to call you "little mouse".

EVAN: Auntie Pearlie, I have to get back to work. If I'm gone more than an hour, the whole place falls apart.

PEARLIE: Take some candies with you. Here, put them in your pockets. Little mouse.

The second I walk in she starts clutching her purse like it's a life preserver. She had the thing in a death hold by the time I left.

First I had to explain who the hell I was talking about a good three dozen times. "Elvis Presley?" she kept asking, like maybe I was doing a documentary on Elvis Shapiro, the Toronto proctologist.

I wasted a whole afternoon eating butter cookies and looking through her wedding album singing "Heartbreak Hotel."

In the end, she limps into her bedroom and comes back with a sweaty little yellow envelope.

"Don't think your Auntie Pearlie doesn't love you," she says.

I've got to call my mother.

The Jewish Y—
Two weeks later, Evan and Ari in the steam bath

EVAN: I get into the building elevator, rip open the envelope and there's eighteen fucking dollars inside. Old cow. Eighteen stinking dollars!
ARI: Shit. Hey, let's go for smoked meat.
EVAN: You're worse than Pearlie. I don't eat flesh.

Evan tries to recruits his best friend Jonathan to come on the Elvis film shoot

JONATHAN: Why exactly do you need me?
EVAN: I like having you around. You can come up with ideas.
You'll be my idea man.
JONATHAN: You're talking crazy talk.
EVAN: Jon, what else do you have going on? It'll be fun. Like going on trips when you were a kid.
JONATHAN: I hated going on trips when I was a kid.
EVAN: Look, I don't know why I have to twist your arm about this.
You should be happy.
JONATHAN: Happy to be crammed into a Winnebago for a week with a bunch of strangers and a Chassidic Elvis impersonator? What do you think this is? The Rolling Thunder Review?
EVAN: There's a per diem.
JONATHAN: How much?
EVAN: Thirty-five American dollars a day.
JONATHAN: Will I have to crap in that Winnebago toilet? Because I refuse to do that. You'll have to stop.
EVAN: I'll stop.
JONATHAN: I don't want an argument every time, either.
EVAN: I'll stop.
JONATHAN: Promise?
EVAN: I'll stop.

Evan goes to Aunt Pearlie again to beg for money. This time he brings along Jonathan.

Jonathan's notes towards a novel he will never finish

"What have I ever asked you for?" says Evan.

"You don't stop asking. You need a healthy dose of shame," says Pearlie.

"That's true. You have no shame," says Jonathan, sitting at the kitchen table. There's a deck of cards next to the salt shaker and he's fighting back the temptation to pick his teeth with the two of clubs. Pearlie's brisket was wonderful.

"Please," yells Evan.

"My God. It's like I'm in a Yiddish opera," says Pearlie.

Jonathan gets more Jell-O with the bits of cantaloupe from the fridge.

"Why does it have to become an opera?" asks Evan.

Pearlie makes a face. A face of distaste. A face her husband used to find beautiful, may his soul rest in peace.

"Why not a short and to-the-point music video?" Jonathan asks.

Evan ignores him. At this point, he can tune Jonathan out like an old pro.

"What do you want from me?" asks Pearlie.

"Evan?" asks Jonathan.

"I want," says Evan looking at both his Auntie and his best friend, "to change the course of Jewish history."

Evan's dedication in Jonathan's high school yearbook

Ah Jon! Jon, ya gaddamn matzo factory worker. Well, it's been a long hard struggle up this toilet bowl of life but we're finally graduating from this penitentiary. I wish you continued success and hope you get "F'd" real soon and I mean real soon. Anyways, take care.

Evan on his cell phone

Oh my God. Auntie Pearlie, this is going to make such a difference. I knew you would realize . . . Do you know what this means? Thank God. Thank the Lord. Auntie Pearlie . . . what can I say? This is very special. No, I mean it. You're going to get every last penny back from me, so help me God. Auntie Pearlie, you're a real friend and that means a lot.

What Pearlie's thinking

dada yayeh
didi yehyeh
nananyadadayee

Oye.
Abie if you were alive.

tidayadeedadee

You should be
holding a chair for me
by the sweet table.

yadadee

You should see
what the world
is now.

dayadedaadee

I'm so tired.

"We have the money. Get us a director. Let's make history."

(Ari recruits Max Wallace as Director.)

Ari's message left on Max's answering machine:

Dude! Hey man. It's Ari Cohen. Hope everything's okay, man. I was just thinking of you because I got something coming up that might be cool. I'm not sure. I'd like to talk, so call me as soon as you can. I'll tell you this much: it's about a movie. Yeah! Dude, I think I'm making a movie, so we definitely got to talk. I'll say this much for now: It involves Elvis, Jews, Jewish Elvis. . . . Max, are you sitting down? Sit down, Max. Elvis is a Jew. Elvis is a freaking Jew. I shit you not, home-grown. How's that? I know. You're thinking, "who gives a shit," right? That's what I thought, but there are thousands of little old Jewish women who grew up on this Elvis and they're sitting in darkened cinemas, chewing Freedent and just waiting for this film — our film — to be made. Oh yeah, we've got money. Get back to me man. Hope to talk soon. Ciao.

Max leaves a message on production company answering machine:

Hey Ari, nice of you to think of me. I got to say, I don't know about this. But one thing's for sure, if you're going to have a movie that revolves around a quest, you're going to need a central figure — a main character people can relate to. Every film from *Cannonball Run* to *Follow That Bird* has a quest. I got the perfect guy for you. He performs under the name "Schmelvis." He's an authentic, born-again Chassidic Jew with a beard and everything. He does Jewish songs like "Hava Nagila"and "Simen Tov" and "Mazel Tov" in an Elvis style, mainly in old age homes and stuff like that. He told me he always had this spiritual connection with Elvis Presley, even though I doubt he knows Elvis was a Jew. He's a nice guy. I met him when my grandmother was at the Jewish nursing home. My *bubbe* really liked him. Think about it. It'll help things. I'm not sure exactly how. Let's feel him out.

Evan on Max:

He's a string bean of a guy tall enough to block out the rednecks and a fast enough talker to get us out of trouble. He's an investigative journalist and he's like a walking encyclopedia of pop culture. Last time I saw him he droned on and on for, like, two hours. My ears almost fell off, but he had some pretty interesting things to say. As long as he keeps his yap shut.

Max on Evan and Ari:

I met them at a festival in Vermont. They were pretending to be French, from France, to pick up chicks. Bad French accents and berets. What a couple of schmucks.

Auntie Pearlie's kitchen — Evan munches on a carrot stick

EVAN: You know what Elvis's favorite meal was? Fried peanut butter and banana sandwiches.
PEARLIE: Why not?
EVAN: He liked it all fried up in pig grease.
PEARLIE: Feh.
EVAN: It's true. That's how . . .
PEARLIE: Stop it. I'm going to throw up.

Makes about 6 cups; 12-14 large balls

Beat on medium speed for 1 minute:
    4 large eggs
    1 teaspoon salt

Stir in: 1/2 cup finely diced fennel, 2 tablespoons snipped fresh dill
and 4 teaspoons snipped fresh or dried chives

Stir in: 1/3 cup plus 1 tablespoon soda water

Fold in until well blended:
    1 cup matzo meal
    1/4 teaspoon ground black pepper
    1-2 teaspoons finely chopped peeled fresh ginger

Cover and refrigerate for 1-4 hours.

With wet hands, form the matzo balls. Drop the balls into a large pot of boiling salted water, cover, reduce the heat, and simmer for 20 minutes. When the matzo balls are almost ready, heat 6 cups chicken stock in a soup pot.

Season with salt and black pepper.

Add the matzo balls to stock. Ladle the stock into warmed bowls and add 2 matzo balls each.

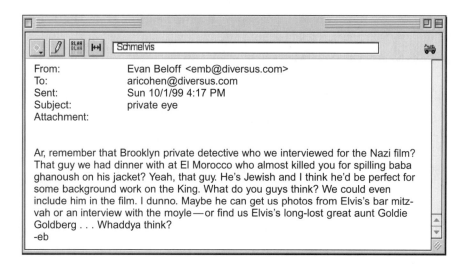

From: Evan Beloff <emb@diversus.com>
To: aricohen@diversus.com
Sent: Sun 10/1/99 4:17 PM
Subject: private eye
Attachment:

Ar, remember that Brooklyn private detective who we interviewed for the Nazi film? That guy we had dinner with at El Morocco who almost killed you for spilling baba ghanoush on his jacket? Yeah, that guy. He's Jewish and I think he'd be perfect for some background work on the King. What do you guys think? We could even include him in the film. I dunno. Maybe he can get us photos from Elvis's bar mitzvah or an interview with the moyle—or find us Elvis's long-lost great aunt Goldie Goldberg . . . Whaddya think?
-eb

Vision for the film: Every documentary needs a central character. Elvis is dead, so that leaves us with a void. Schmelvis is the perfect character to substitute for the King. I figure we take him down south, dress him up in a full-style Elvis Las Vegas jumpsuit covered with Stars of David instead of American Stars and Stripes and let him loose on the Elvis fans, fundamentalist Christians, and white-trash rednecks. We could go down Highway 61 in a Winnebago—"The Winnebagel!"—stopping in truck stops, diners, and trailer parks, pushing him out and filming the fun.

Every August in Memphis they have a commemoration of Elvis's death. Thousands of Elvis fanatics, freaks, and impersonators descend on Graceland to pay tribute to the King. If we time our trip right, we can arrive just in time to capture the craziness. They'll love Schmelvis down there, especially when he tells them with a straight face all about Elvis's Jewish side.

While we're there, we can conduct a genuine search for Elvis's Jewish roots, interviewing friends, family members, and the like to see whether he ever mentioned Judaism. We can head down to his birthplace and see if there are any Jews there who might know something.

We'd have to make sure the film doesn't turn into a mockumentary. If it's going to get attention, people have to believe Elvis was really Jewish.

To: Max Wallace, Diversus Productions
From: Steven Rambam, Private Investigator, New York City

The following, as you requested, represents the results of my initial investigation into Elvis Presley's Jewish roots, his family background, and any evidence that Elvis may have practiced Judaism:

The earliest known roots on Elvis's mother's side are actually Cherokee Indian stemming from his great-great-great-grandmother, Morning White Dove (1800-1835). At the time it was common for male settlers in the West to marry "white" Indians as there was a scarcity of females on the American frontier. In 1818, she married William Mansell, a settler in western Tennessee. William's father, Richard Mansell, had been a soldier in the Revolutionary War. The Mansells migrated from Norman France to Scotland, and then later to Ireland. In the eighteenth century the family came to the American Colonies. William Mansell and Morning White Dove had three children, the eldest of whom was John Mansell, born in 1828, who was Elvis's great-great-grandfather.

In 1880 John Mansell moved to Oxford, Mississippi and changed his name to Colonel Lee Mansell. His sons left Hamilton to seek their fortunes in the town of Saltillo, Mississippi, near Tupelo, the birthplace of Elvis Presley. The third of John Mansell's sons, White Mansell, became the patriarch of the family when John moved to Oxford. White Mansell was Elvis's great-grandfather.

White Mansell married Martha Tackett, a neighbor in Saltillo, on Jan. 22, 1870. Her mother was Nancy Burdine, who, according to Elvis's third cousin, Oscar Tackett, was a full-blooded Jew. Very little is known about the Burdines, although they probably came from Lithuania around the time of the American Revolution. According to Oscar Tackett, two of Martha's brothers, Sidney and Jerome, had Jewish names. In the eighteenth and nineteenth centuries, the American South experienced a significant migration of European Jews who settled in the southern states to open up dry goods and general merchandise stores, although some of them took up farming. By the middle of the eighteenth century, a Jewish family operated nearly every general store in the south.

During the Civil War, there were so many Jews fighting for the Confederate army that General Lee couldn't permit Jewish soldiers to refrain from fighting on Saturdays, the Jewish Sabbath. By the end of the war, between 5,000-10,000 Jews had been killed in the fighting, significantly reducing the southern Jewish population.

Because her mother, Nancy Burdine, was a Jew, Martha Tackett (Elvis's great-grandmother) was also Jewish. According to Jewish law, the religion is passed on matrilineally (on the mother's side). It is likely that Martha Tackett converted to Christianity when she married White Mansell. However, biblical law would still consider her to be Jewish.

In 1876, Martha gave birth in Saltillo, Mississippi to a daughter, Octavia Luvenia (Doll) Mansell, Elvis's grandmother. On September 20, 1903, Doll Mansell married Bob Smith. Nine years later, the couple had a daughter, Gladys Love Smith, Elvis's mother. Because she was descended matrilineally from Nancy Burdine, the Jewish ancestor, Gladys was also Jewish. So, when she gave birth to Elvis Aron Presley in Tupelo, Mississippi on Jan 8, 1935, her son was a full-blooded Jew, according to laws dating back more than 4,000 years.

The Presleys were devout Christians. Each Sunday they attended the Assembly of God Church in Tupelo and there is no question that Elvis was brought up as a God-fearing Christian. I am still determining when Elvis first learned of his Jewish roots. His mother, Gladys, died in 1959 while Elvis was in Germany with the U.S. Army. His father Vernon made the arrangements and buried Gladys at Forest Hills Cemetery with a headstone bearing a Christian crucifix. However, around 1970, Elvis made arrangements to have a Jewish Star of David added to the headstone along with the cross.

In 1972, Elvis appeared on stage at a performance in Salt Lake City, Utah wearing a Jewish *chai* pendant of the Jewish symbol of life around his neck. When he was found dead of a heart attack in the bathroom of his Graceland home on August 16, 1977, the *chai* necklace was around his neck. In 1974, he was asked by a reporter why he wore a Jewish *chai* and he responded, "I don't want to be left out of Heaven on a technicality." Elvis's *chai* pendant is actually displayed on the Graceland tour in a glass display case, although there is no mention of his Jewish roots.

In 1973, Elvis commissioned sixteen gold watches from a Memphis jeweler named Harry Levitch and distributed one to each member of his Memphis Mafia, the entourage who traveled with him. The watches had an unusual feature. Each one flashed an alternating symbol of a crucifix and a Star of David.

When Elvis died in 1977, he was first buried in Memphis's Forest Hills Cemetery beside his mother but, two years later, his father Vernon had both graves moved to the back garden of his Graceland mansion. When his mother's gravestone was moved to Graceland, the headstone bearing the Star of David did not accompany it and so the millions of tourists who come to Graceland every year do not see this compelling evidence of Elvis's Jewish roots.

So far, we have only the account of Elvis's cousin Oscar Tackett to confirm that his great-great-great-grandmother was Jewish. I can provide you with documented evidence but it will be expensive. I will have to travel to Tupelo and Jackson, Mississippi to uncover her birth records and her death certificate or a gravestone bearing a Star of David. Please inform me whether you can afford such an undertaking. It will cost approximately $25,000.

p.s. According to Elvis's death certificate, he was not circumcised.

To: Steven Rambam
From: Max Wallace

Thanks for the report, Steve. But what if we can't afford your fee? What happens if we don't have that kind of money?

To: Max Wallace
From: Steve Rambam

Then Steve Rambam has left the building!

Morning White Dove (b.1800)
William Mansell (m.1818)

Octavia Luvenia
(Doll) Mansell

White Mansell
Martha Tackett

Bob Smith

Vernon Presley
Gladys Love Smith

John Mansell (b.1828)
Nancy Burdine

Elvis

Scenario involving Elvis and an imagined Jewish past

GLADYS: *Elveleh,* when you go out, would you pick up a *chalah* and some *Shabbos* candles? Be a doll and come back and massage your poor mama's feet.
ELVIS: All right, *mameh.*

Doing first shoot today on Elvis film. We're meeting Schmelvis to enlist him for the project. Max wants to do it at Bens Deli because the famous sixties Leonard Cohen documentary was shot there and he says it's loaded with Jewish character. Two of the waiters who served Cohen in 1965 are still working there so maybe we'll get something out of that. I just found out that Schmelvis is actually an ultra-ultra-Orthodox Jew, a member of one of the Chassidic sects. This could be weird.

1. MONTREAL. BENS DELICATESSEN, THE COUNTER.

JONATHAN and EVAN meet SCHMELVIS for breakfast at the kitsch 1960s diner with autographed celebrity photos adorning every inch of tacky wall space. They are seated at the counter.

EVAN (*to Schmelvis*): What are you having for breakfast?
SCHMELVIS: Are you talking to me? I can't eat anything. It's not kosher. I'll just have a coffee in a Styrofoam cup.
EVAN: How are we going to get through this trip if we have to find kosher restaurants wherever we go? Jonathan, will you talk to him?
JONATHAN: Ever eat bacon?
SCHMELVIS: Not really.
JON: When you say not really . . .
SCHMELVIS: I've smelled it.
JONATHAN: I think it's time you tried some and then made any decisions about religion from there.
SCHMELVIS: Ach, God forbid.
JONATHAN: Never a little tempted? In the middle of the night? No one around?
SCHMELVIS: I have no interest. It smells horrible.
JONATHAN: Now I know you're putting me on. Everyone likes the smell of bacon. Even pigs like the smell of bacon.
SCHMELVIS: Well, when the *Moschiach* [the Messiah] comes, then we can eat bacon.
EVAN: Imagine that, eh? All these holy rabbis sitting down to a big plate of pork and beans.
JONATHAN: That's what Judaism's really all about . . . our triumph over bacon.
SCHMELVIS: Not to complain, but we could have met at a kosher restaurant.
JONATHAN: What Jew doesn't like Bens?
EVAN: Yeah. You don't see me complaining about the beard hair you're shedding all over the counter.

(*A WAITER in his sixties passes a rag over the counter.*)

WAITER: What are you having?
EVAN: I'm not eating. Jon, have your plate of bacon.
JONATHAN: I can't eat bacon sitting next to him. (*pointing to Schmelvis*) I'll have a smoked meat. I'm the only person eating?
EVAN: I'm vegan.
JONATHAN: Congratulations.
SCHMELVIS: I've got some benchers [prayer books] in the trunk of my car. After we eat, we're going to elevate this place.
EVAN: How can you elevate the place any more than it already is? Leonard Cohen's peed in the urinals.
SCHMELVIS: I feel like I'm eating in a urinal.

EVAN: You know, Schmel, what are you going to do when we're on the road in the States and someone invites you in for homemade apple pie?

SCHMELVIS: I'll tell you exactly what I'll do. I'll take it, thank them, and put my fork into it, but I won't eat it.

EVAN: Oh yes you will. You can't refuse their southern hospitality. It would be rude. You can at least take a bite.

SCHMELVIS: Not going to happen.

JONATHAN: I think we'll be needing an apple pie spittoon.

(*The WAITER clears away the dishes.*)

EVAN: Dan, do you realize what this'll mean if you can actually prove that Elvis was a Jew? They'll instantly make you the grand poohbah of *Chassidic* Jewry for your *halachic* investigation.

JONATHAN: Is there some kind of hierarchy at work, some kind of allotment of points depending on who you turn up as Jewish? Or is it all the same? Is a Jew a Jew? Like, is Elvis worth more than the guy who played the landlord on *Three's Company*?

MAX (*from behind the camera*): I think he's already Jewish.

JONATHAN: He probably is.

EVAN: Which one? Mr. Roper or Mr. Furley?

JONATHAN: Probably both.

EVAN: Really?

JONATHAN: All I'm asking is how does this all work?

EVAN: Is Norman Fell really Jewish?

(*Pause.*)

JONATHAN: Are we doing a documentary about Norman Fell?
(*Jonathan takes a bite out of his smoked meat. Evan looks disgusted. Schmelvis stirs the coffee in his Styrofoam cup.*)

SCHMELVIS: Do you think Elvis was circumcised?

EVAN: Ask one of the twenty thousand women he banged. We should all be so lucky.

(*The MANAGER of Bens, doing paperwork at a nearby table, comes over.*)

MANAGER: My brother's the world's biggest Elvis fan. He told me he read in a book that Elvis wasn't circumcised.

(*He calls over his BROTHER, who's setting up tables.*)

BROTHER: What's all this about Elvis's penis?

EVAN: Was it circumcised?

BROTHER: It wasn't, according to that Albert Goldman biography, and you know what? He never liked his penis. He was ashamed of it. It wasn't like his friends'.

EVAN: So he didn't like his dick because it wasn't snipped. How do you know this stuff?

BROTHER: I read books. It's funny. I always remembered that. It just stuck in my head. He just wanted his penis to be more Jewish. (laughing) Well, that's a little snippet for you, if you'll pardon the expression.

EVAN: Well, if he didn't like his penis, he's got a lot in common with other Jewish men.

JONATHAN: Or the girlfriends of Jewish men.

BROTHER: He found it ugly. That's the word he used.

EVAN (to Jonathan and Schmelvis): Do you find your penis ugly?

BROTHER (walking away): I haven't even served my first smoked meat yet today and already I'm talking about penises.

[FILM STILL OF BENS, PREFERABLY AN OUTSIDE SHOT OF THE RESTAURANT]

SCHMELVIS: If I go on this trip, it's to bring Yiddishkite to people. That's what's really important to me. More important than Elvis any day.

EVAN: Hey, this whole thing is all about Yiddishkite. We're going to say Kaddish, the Jewish prayer for the dead, at Elvis's grave.

SCHMELVIS: Look, you can't mess around with Kaddish, if that's what you're talking about. That's no joke. Certain laws have to be observed.

EVAN: What laws?

SCHMELVIS: Like for instance, you need ten Jewish men to form a minyan for when you say Kaddish.

EVAN: So? Big deal. We'll get ten men. Big deal. They'll have to do it free, though, because I'm not paying any more people.

SCHMELVIS: And they have to all be Jewish.

EVAN: Jesus Christ. You know what, Dan? You're never happy.

SCHMELVIS: These are the days of revelation. Our deeds will bring down the Moschiach. We're going to give the man a proper consecration. Not even one Jewish soul should go lost.

EVAN: That's the attitude! See? Now we're talking about something important. If Elvis is Jewish, then we'll bring down the messiah, right? That's what you're telling me, right?

SCHMELVIS: Not exactly.

EVAN: But something like that?

SCHMELVIS: Something like that.

Schmelvis on his cell phone with his wife

I'm paying $15/week for an ad in the newspaper that no one cares about. The way I see it, this whole film is one long advertising campaign for me. After people see this thing, I'll be booked up every weekend. They're buying me outfits and whatnot. Don't ask. And I'll tell you something else; it might help to spread a little Yid-dishkite. What's wrong with that? They don't seem like bad guys either. I'm thinking I could use a little fun . . . of course I have fun with you. Don't be like that.

Evan's Production Journal

Shit. We're going to have to eat in kosher restaurants. Jonathan says, "You're ransacking the Jewish culture for film ideas. The least you can do is force-feed yourself a lousy white fish sandwich."

Max played me one of Schmelvis's videos from the old age home. It's absurd. It's like Andy Kaufman meets Jackie Mason.

2. MONTREAL, ISRAEL BETH AARON SYNAGOGUE, HALLWAY.

Schmelvis and Evan stop outside the office door of Evan's rabbi. A sign reads: "RABBI REUBEN POUPKO."

SCHMELVIS: What's he like?
EVAN: Like Herschel Krustovsky, you know, Krusty the Clown on *The Simpsons*. Chain-smoking, wisecracking. He'll love this project.

SYNAGOGUE, RABBI POUPKO'S OFFICE.

RABBI POUPKO (*shakes Evan's hand*): Who's this?
EVAN: That's Schmelvis.
RABBI: He's an Elvis impersonator? He doesn't look like Elvis. If he's an Elvis impersonator, I can be Robert Redford's impersonator.
SCHMELVIS: You haven't heard the schtick yet, Rabbi. (*goes into an Elvis pose and starts to sing*) "Since my matzo ball left me..."
RABBI: Close the door, this is embarrassing!
EVAN: I'm in over my head, Rabbi. I need spiritual counsel. Do you think this has significance, this thing that I'm trying to do?
RABBI (*feet up on his desk*): What are you trying to do?
EVAN: I'm not sure.
SCHMELVIS: We're going to say *Kaddish* for Elvis.
RABBI: Assuming he's Jewish. It's his great-grandmother, on the mother's side, who was Jewish? It's on the mother's side, right, it's all mothers?
EVAN: He's Jewish, he's Jewish. He better be Jewish. Do you know how screwed I am if that redneck bastard isn't? It's important that he's Jewish, right? It makes a point of some kind, doesn't it?

RABBI: The point? I'll say this: If Elvis is Jewish—and if he was, he didn't do a thing about it—then he's an allegory for the plight of the Diaspora Jew. If you decide to marry a non-Jew, then three generations down the line, your great grandson is Elvis—a guy without a clue that he comes from Jewish stock. Do you think that's significant? Do you think being Jewish is significant? If you do, then the story of Elvis is a lesson for every Jew alive today.

SCHMELVIS: That's why we need a rabbi to make this kosher. That's why we need you, Rabbi. Are you up for the mission?

RABBI: Am I up for the mission? I don't know. It's interesting, but do you think the gentiles down in the South will think we're kidnapping their boy?

EVAN: That's fascinating in itself. Any other conspiracies you want to weave into it about Judaism you can.

Evan calls Ari on his cell phone

I'm very inspired. We're doing good work here, Ar. And the Rabbi's coming with us to Memphis. But he refuses to even set foot into the Winnebago. He agreed to come only if I fly him down and get him his own hotel room and rent him an air-conditioned Caddy.

Ari, we need him. He dignifies the project. Without him, we're just a bunch of dorks. We're a five-minute segment on *Real People*.

Director's Log, Dec. 13, 1999

We shot a scene today at the office of Rabbi Reuben Poupko. We were just supposed to get a rabbinical perspective on the Elvis is Jewish angle, sort of the blessing of the Jewish community. Instead, Schmelvis spontaneously asked the Rabbi if he would come with us to Memphis. And the Rabbi said yes. Of course, there were a few conditions. He refuses to ride down with us on the Winnebago. We have to put him up in a nice hotel and rent him an air-conditioned Cadillac. A small price to pay to get him in the film. The guy's the craziest badass rabbi I've ever met. Wait till the South gets a load of him. . . .

It's clear now that the film is going to be a great psychodrama. Already, Evan and Schmelvis are at each other's throats. That's a good excuse to make a film. Better than looking for Elvis's Jewish roots. The trick is to complete the film before these characters kill each other. Goal: self-destruction.

Tomorrow we're taking some faux footage of Auntie Pearlie to make her feel like a movie star. Jonathan says Pearlie's brisket is great. Maybe she'll feed us.

Max takes Dan (sound man)
and Mila (camera man) over to Auntie Pearlie's

PEARLIE: Come in. Come in. Don't worry about your shoes. When the grass is growing out of my ass, the carpet will still be here, you know what I mean, dears? Come in, already. You're letting out the warm. So you want me I should talk about Evan? Well, what do you want to know? About how he lives off lettuce? You're his friend. You know the story. You know my troubles. Tell me, you eat meat? Of course you do. We used to call a man like you a "Big Daddy." Do they still call you that?

DAN: I don't think I've ever been called that.

PEARLIE: Al Capone was a big daddy.

DAN: I think we just say "fat bastard" nowadays.

PEARLIE: No. I don't mean fat, honey. You're a big man. A woman could drape herself across your lap and you could support her.

DAN: Like Santa Claus.

PEARLIE: Oh stop it already. You're making fun.

MAX: So tell us about your relationship with Evan.

PEARLIE: My relationship? I wasn't aware I was in a relationship. Alright, let's see. He's got some mouth on him. He's like Muhammad Ali that way. Except he weighs about 75 pounds. And I have to say something about that haircut.

MAX: What about it?

PEARLIE: *Gott in Himmel!* Have you looked at him? He looks like he just stepped out of a mental clinic. You know my girlfriends in the building think he's retarded. You shouldn't tell him that and give him a complex, but when he walks in, they shake their heads and say such a shame. Tell me, does he have a nipple ring?

MAX (*laughing*): I wouldn't know.

PEARLIE: Oh yeah. Don't worry. I've heard of these things. I bet he has one. Next time he comes over I'm going to make him take off his shirt.

MAX: And how will you do that?

PEARLIE: I'll tell him I bought him some deodorant to try.

Elvis: King of Jerusalem

One of the best known skits in the history of "Saturday Night Live" was a game show parody called "Jew? Not Jew?" in which contestants had to guess which famous show business celebrities were Jewish. Among the surprising list of figures revealed to be Jews were Paul Newman, Robert DeNiro, and Lauren Bacall.

But of all the unlikely celebrities among the Chosen People, one name never surfaced—and if it had, nobody would have believed it — the King of Rock'n'Roll, Elvis Presley. That's because nobody knew Elvis was Jewish until the influential *Wall Street Journal* published an article in 1998, "All Shook Up in the Holy Land," exposing the King's improbable lineage.

The *Wall Street Journal* revelation provides the backdrop for the 90-minute off-beat documentary *Elvis: King of Jerusalem*.

The focus of the film is a true-life Montreal-based Jewish Elvis impersonator, Schmelvis. For years he has worked as an entertainer at Jewish senior citizens' homes singing his own versions of Elvis songs in a Jewish musical style.

Our cameras follow Schmelvis on a bizarre odyssey, which forms the core of the film. When Schmelvis finds out Elvis is Jewish, he decides to embark on a single-minded journey. He is determined to travel to Elvis's Graceland home in Memphis to say Kaddish—the Jewish prayer for the dead—at Elvis's grave. When he arrives in Memphis, he attempts to recruit nine Jewish men to form minyan—the traditional ten men needed to elevate someone's soul to God.

His trip down America's legendary Highway 61 in a Winnebago will provide our cameras with hilarious fodder. Stopping at roadside diners along the way, Schmelvis will mingle with the cast of characters who populate such establishments—rednecks, truckers, white trash, and middle Americans. As Schmelvis tries to convince his fellow travelers that Elvis was a Jew, their reactions will provide bizarre and unpredictable material, which should leave audiences in stitches.

Schmelvis will arrive at Graceland in early August—the anniversary of the King's death—in time for "Elvis Week," the annual pilgrimage when thousands of fans and Elvis impersonators descend on Memphis to pay tribute to their idol. His encounters with these Elvis worshippers are sure to be equally entertaining.

In between the comical moments of documenting Schmelvis's odyssey, the film will intersperse very serious footage to provide an entertaining contrast.

Among the footage:
- A solemn Rabbi explaining Jewish matrilineal law to confirm that Elvis was indeed officially Jewish.
- Scenes contrasting a Jewish cantor singing in a synagogue and concert footage of Elvis singing in a surprisingly similar style.
- A university Cultural Studies professor describing the universal significance of Elvis.
- A religious scholar will explain that many Elvis gospel songs, which his fans have always believed prove his devotion to Christianity, are actually descended from the Old Testament and have very strong Jewish roots.
- An interview with the *Wall Street Journal* reporter who broke the story.
- An interview with Graceland spokesperson Todd Morgan, who will discuss Elvis's knowledge of his historical roots.

The combination of comical episodes with very serious and solemn footage will be quite amusing in itself. However, we will go to great lengths to ensure that the film does not devolve into farce and does not mock Judaism in any way.

Title: Elvis: King of Jerusalem
Duration: 90 minutes
Format: super 16-mm film, digital video
Locations: United States

Production schedule: January-September 2000
Post-production: October-November 2000

Evan's Journal

I really believe this is about destiny. It chose me. The film will promote unity. I mean, here's this guy, he's a cultural icon, and I think if people could see that he's Jewish, then maybe that would go a long way to destroying a lot of hurtful stereotypes.

I mean, maybe some guy out there who doesn't really know a thing about Jews, who thinks we have horns and tails, I mean if a guy like that can be reached and shown that not only are Jews like anyone else, they can also be Elvis. He's someone no one could have ever seen as a Jew in a million years. It might even change the way he's perceived, the way Jews are seen.

Jonathan keeps saying: "We're making this film for anti-Semites. We're thinking of calling it ELVIS IS A JEW: PLEASE DON'T HATE US." But he's a jack-ass with no understanding of history. If I really think about it, it doesn't mean a goddamn thing that Elvis is a Jew. Shit: If he were born in Europe instead of America, he would have been thrown into the ovens. The Nazis used the same criteria we use to distinguish the Jew from the gentile. It's not an arbitrary point who your great-grandmother was. The Nazis traced Jewish lineage through the matrilineal line the same way Jews do. Elvis would have been just as dead as a Chassidic Jew.

The well dressed Elvis

Rick Marino, author of *Be Elvis! A Guide to Impersonating Elvis Presley*, recommends buying Simplicity Costumes Pattern 8646. The jumpsuit requires at least six yards of polyester gabardine and two yards of polyester satin.

Jonathan's Journal

Evan's always dragging me along for one scheme or another. When we were sixteen, he convinced me to spend the summer with him in Wildwood, New Jersey to work on the Boardwalk. We lived in a boarding house in a small room with four other people. The woman who ran the place was charging us each $400 a month. We were sixteen and stupid.

Evan's parents, who drove us down from Montreal, decided the Garfield was a good place for us to stay after having been so utterly charmed by its rustic quaintness (i.e. the dartboard in the foyer and the LIFE magazines on the coffee table). Mr. D.—the "D" stood for something long, Polish and unpronounceable—the all-American, cauliflower-eared, beef-baron owner, told them that he would treat us right and never beat us. His wife was an alcoholic, Mrs. Robinson type, with all of the meanness and none of the sex appeal. Evan said that when she was younger, she must have had a real "bangable bod." Evan had a job all lined up, and I was supposed to get one too, but on our fourth night there, still without work, I sat on the edge of my bed (Evan and I had these Ernie and Bert adjacent cots) and felt that sense of being a failure—a man who is a failure—for the first time. I looked out through our window at The Boardwalk. The big Ferris wheel shimmered in the heat like a big carny Moloch sand dancing in the desert.

Our first night there Evan and I went to see FERRIS BUELLER'S DAY OFF. In the front row, I spread out across three seats so it was all like back home on the couch. After the movie, at an arcade, I tried to bang these pop-up little weasel heads with a colorful plastic hammer. I hit about half of them and won three tickets. I traded them for a little propeller hat that fit on my thumb and a plastic cigarette with a cherry at the tip that looked almost real. On the way back to the Garfield, I drew two dots for eyes on my thumb and with the hat on, I made it talk in a squeaky female voice into Evan's ear. I was beginning to feel fine.

All we ever talked about that summer was how badly we had to get laid. My most glorious prospect was a girl named Denise who lived in our boarding house. She had puffy orange hair and worked in an ice-cream parlor.

"Today someone called me 'Sir,' she said.

"Ah, come on. It must have been some senile old man, right?"

"It was a young mother. It's the third time it's happened this week."

"Maybe you should wear some eye make-up," I said.

"I can't. It always starts to run all over the ice cream like sundae sauce."

The day I left the Garfield to go home to Montreal, she gave me this long kiss on the lips that really freaked me out and had Evan in stitches.

It should be said that there is a special tang to the lustful pang you feel for a girl in the summer when you share a boarding house at the age of sixteen. Everything looks so good, it's like a big, sexy, incestuous love boat slowly sinking into the autumn.

Now we were about to embark on another trip in a Winnebago and we were men and we had other problems. There was no more school to begin. We were no longer sinking into the autumn. We were sinking into something that no one had even given a name yet.

Part 2

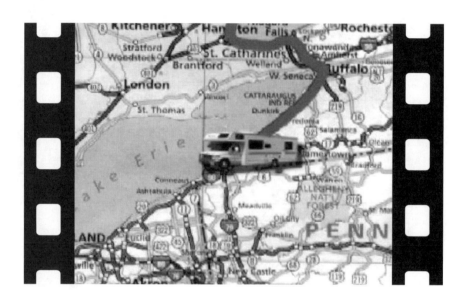

Director's Log, Aug. 11, 2000

Why a Winnebago? Because it'll fit us all comfortably. Because it'll be fun. Because everyone can goof around, take showers on the road. Frolic. And it'll look great in the film. All the guys running around, Ari basting a chicken, Evan coming out of the shower with a towel wrapped around his waist. It's these little details that will make the film a sort of *Blair Witch Project* with some Elvis and a little Yiddishkite thrown in to boot. It'll be a screwball comedy with a heart.

SUN COAST RV — THE MINNIE WINNIE

Such a pleasure to drive, and so easy to own: the Winnebago Minnie. Some companies strive to meet your expectations. At Winnebago Industries, we aim to exceed them. And such is the case with our Winnebago Minnie — a Class C motor home that's loaded with features you'd expect to find in more expensive motor homes.

You can immediately see the quality and sense the value we've brought to the Minnie Winnie as you notice the richness of its oak cabinetry, which features a catalyzed finish typically found in the kitchens of finer homes. Less noticeable — but equally valuable — are smart design features such as ceiling-ducted air conditioning, for improved interior comfort. We've thought through all the details, from attractive Stitchcraft furniture all the way to our one-piece fiberglass roof, which provides strength, durability and long-lasting good looks.

And with so many choices, you'll be sure to find a Minnie that's just right for you.

Ari's first poem written in the Winnebago

Unititled

We pick up Schmelvis at his house.
He gets on smelling like Kung Fu aftershave.
Evan looks out the window, brushes his hair back.
Mila films Schmelvis's entrance with Max's
chin practically resting on his shoulder.

Schmelvis smiles for whatever he is
in that house
he is now the center of attention.

He starts loading tins of sardines into the cupboard,
"Like this I'm good for the whole week."
Evan turns away from the window,
"Great! All we needed were sardine farts."

Schmelvis smiles. He's wearing Elvis shades.
He's decided to be cool.
Max's decided to be professional.
Evan's decided to be nervous.
And I've decided to watch from a careful distance.

VITAMINS:
ESSENTIAL FATTY ACIDS
SAW PALMETTO
VITAMIN C
VITAMIN E
SPIRULINA POWDER WITH SPRING WATER

BARBECUED TOFU
WHOLE GRAIN BREAD
SPELT BREAD
SPROUTS
HUMMUS
BUNNY LOVE BABY CARROTS
ORGANIC UNSALTED RICE CAKES
SOY POWER SHAKES - CHOCOLATE
GRANOLA BARS
FLAX SEED MEGA BREAKFAST BARS
VANILLA SOY MILK
BACON TOFU SLICES
POWER PUFFS - GINSENG FLAVORED
VEGGIE BOOTY - GREEN
ORGANIC PEACHES AND ORANGES

*The Winnebago is just outside the Montreal city limits, the green
highway signs visible through the windows. Schmelvis wraps tfillin
(Jewish ritual leather straps used every morning as the men say a
prayer). He lays them down on the kitchen table.*

SCHMELVIS: Who's next? Evan? Come over here.

(EVAN is laying on the couch reading a Johnny Cash biography.)

EVAN (*not looking away from the book*): Don't even start. Is this
what I have to look forward to? Every goddam sunrise, I'm going to
be greeted by you trying to hog-tie me for the Lord, trying to
bring Yiddishkite to the Winnebagoed masses?
ARI: Hey, I'll put on *tfillin*. Why not?
SCHMELVIS: That's a good man.
EVAN: And I'm a bad Jew, right? I'm not paying you to proselytize.
And why aren't you in the Schmelvis suit? We're going to need to
have some pictures of you eating poutine at a roadside diner
before we leave the province. Suit up!
SCHMELVIS: Hey, buddy, first of all I don't eat poutine. Second of
all, it's 100 degrees out there.
EVAN: Why isn't the air conditioning on?
MAX (*from up front driving*): It's broken.
EVAN (*finally looking up from his book to stare at the ceiling*):
You realize we're all completely screwed.

I'm not sure this was such a good idea. They all hate me. The Winnebago seemed bigger in the showroom with just me and Max in it.

I think he broke the air conditioning himself, just to up the tension for the film. This thing is like HEART OF DARKNESS without the APOCALYPSE NOW.

I hate them all.

Small talk in the RV

MAX: In the 1968 comeback special, Elvis actually had to be stitched into his leather outfit. How do you get into yours?

SCHMELVIS: I do up the zipper.

MAX: Would you ever stitch yourself into an outfit?

SCHMELVIS: Never.

MAX: Let's say you had to. For TV.

SCHMELVIS: I'm claustrophobic. What if I had to take a leak?

MAX: They'd cut you open.

SCHMELVIS: Down there they're going to cut me open? Forget it.

The thing about driving a Winnebago is that you look in the rearview mirror expecting to see the road behind you, but what you see is a whole bunch of men sitting at a table playing cards. If you're feeling a little vulnerable, seeing cars driving behind you at night can make you kind of paranoid. But seeing men playing cards behind you can make you feel like it's a chronological rear view, a view from a time when you were happy and quiet.

Max is interviewed at a college radio station near Niagara Falls

INTERVIEWER: Have you always been a big Elvis fan?

MAX: I can't stand him.

INTERVIEWER: Are you a religious Jew?

MAX: Actually, I'm an atheist.

INTERVIEWER: So why the film?

MAX: I'm doing it for the money.

WINNEBAGO, LIVING ROOM AREA/COUCH.

Visible through a window, a road sign, "Ohio," followed by a Wendy's, then another sign: "Trust Jesus, Our Only Hope." A red Toyota pick-up speeds by the Winnebago. A man wearing a cut-off shirt sits on a lawn chair in the back of the truck in the open air.

At an intersection, the Winnebago turns in the direction of a Kentucky Fried Chicken road sign.

MAX (*to Schmelvis*): I'm not telling you to go in there and sing "Love Me Fucking Tender." I'm saying, just go in there as Schmelvis and let people check you out while Mila films their reactions. We need some reaction shots. Plus, I'm starving to death. Don't bust my balls. Just get out there with the goddam suit and make me proud.
SCHMELVIS: First of all, it's not even the matter of the suit. What really gets to me is the idea of a Jew eating unkosher. That's what's like a knife penetrating to the core of my heart.
EVAN (*from the back room of the Winnebago*): How about my boot penetrating the core of your ass?
SCHMELVIS: You better shut him up. Jew or no Jew, I'm going to beat his head open like a coconut.
MAX: Shut up back there. Listen, I need a reaction shot. It'll be cute. Give them a little of the Schmelvis magic.
EVAN: And get me a bottle of water.

SCHMELVIS (*lunging towards the back room*):
I'll give you a fucking bottle of water!
MAX (*holding him back*): Where the hell is Mila?
DAN: He's driving the fucking Winnebago, Max.
MAX: Pass me the goddamn camera!
DAN: It's in the case.
MAX: How many times do I have to tell you? Never, never keep it in the goddam case! We should always be ready to roll.

I'll try. I just have a low threshhold for all that Hebrew stuff. I feel like I'm back at bar mitzvah lessons when he starts. It makes me all itchy and claustrophobic.

Why Schmelvis became religious

You go through life, it's like you're living in a kitchen cupboard. You know? Under the sink? With the pipes? And then one day, the door opens. And what's out there? A whole kitchen.

I used to be very prone to depression. I wasn't a light guy. I thought about a lot of very horrifying things.

Like death. What happens after it's all done with, when the worms are crawling through your pee hole like the tunnel of love? Where does all the love you had go? All the books you read, all the things you felt?

No. I'm sorry. I knew there had to be more.

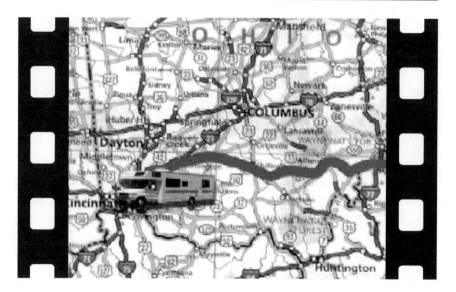

A taste of the Old South

We stop in Melville, Kentucky to fuel up.
A woman at a gas station informs us that when she first arrived in this area, there was a huge Klan rally.
"I've never seen so many hoods," she says.
I tell her about the movie we're making and she tells us that she never met a Jew before.
"What's it like to meet me?" I ask.
"Should I be scared of you?" she says.
I was buying a Chunky chocolate bar. You can't get those in Canada. She was sitting on a chair beside the cash register.
"I don't know a thing about Jews," she says, "but I'll tell you this. I think it's absolutely wrong the way you people were treated. It's just plain wrong to treat folks like that."
She says this in a pure, honest way.

Evan calls Auntie Pearlie from a payphone

PEARLIE: They don't like Jews down there.

EVAN: Where, Auntie Pearlie?

PEARLIE: South, down south. I'm telling you. They don't like Jews in the South.

EVAN: In the South? Where?

PEARLIE: In Kentucky. They don't like Jews. Watch out.

I am the Second Cameraman
a Poem by Ari Cohen

I am the second cameraman

there is an epic unfolding
before the first camera
and then there is the spillage
the parts that are not quite art
but are not worth forfeiting to reality either

they are for me to sweep up
like the guy with the paper bag and dustbin
who follows the elephants at the circus
gathering the refuse
that is still
for the time being anyway
a part of the circus

I capture with my camera
the forgotten lyrical moments:
a woman stripping off her jeans at the beach
Evan fighting with his auntie
on a Kentucky payphone
the hotel clerk pulling dead mice out
from under the fridge

I am the poet who sings
with strep throat

I am the poet who sings
of the stuff the matadors are bored of

Tupelo, Mississippi. Elvis's birthplace.

Rabbi Poupko approaches a motorcycle cop. They stand by a white fire hydrant.

RABBI: What do you think of this sideshow?

COP: I think it's great. I love Elvis.

RABBI: You want to hear something funny? We're doing this movie and the premise of the film is that we found out that Elvis was Jewish.
COP: That's great.
RABBI: You don't have a problem with that?
COP: Nope.
RABBI: He didn't look Jewish to me. Did he look Jewish to you?
COP: Naw.
RABBI: What about me? Do I look Jewish?
COP: Yeah, you look Jewish.
RABBI: What gave it away?

The cop points to the rabbi's yarmulke.

RABBI: That's cheating. Do you think the people of Tupelo like Jews?

COP: Sure.

RABBI: Do you know any Jews yourself?

COP: No, I really don't.

RABBI: Do you have any rabbis here in Tupelo?

COP: I don't think so, but we have some Amish people.

RABBI: Hey hound dog, what percentage of the United States do you think is Jewish?

COP: I'd say about twenty-five percent. Is that a good guess?

RABBI: Naw, it's a good thing we didn't put any money on it. You know what percentage of the United States is Jewish? Less than two percent. We just have big mouths.

COP: Yeah. And a lot of money.

RABBI: He says Jews have a lot of money. (pulls out his wallet) Who's got money on them? All I've got is Canadian. That doesn't really count.

LAKEVIEW MOBILE HOME PARK, PARKING LOT.

Max tries to convince the Rabbi to board the Winnebago.

MAX: We just need a scene of you frolicking with the boys.
RABBI: A man of my spiritual pedigree frolicking? I'd rather frolic in a septic tank. I'm sure it smells horrible in there.
MAX: For five minutes. We'll spray it with Lysol before you get on.
RABBI: I'm not going on that Winnebago. There's no way in hell I'm going on that Winnebago.

(CUT to the Rabbi sitting in the Winnebago.)

JONATHAN: (*lying on the couch eating slices of processed cheese*) Rabbi, if I knew we were having guests, I would have put out the good plastic cutlery.
RABBI: Let me tell you something about Winnebagos. Winnebagos are no place for Jewish boys. Where do you find Winnebagos? In trailer parks. And what happens in trailer parks? Tornados are directed by God to attack trailer parks. It's just a rule of nature. Jews have their own form of suffering. We have pogroms and anti-Semites, but not tornados. Gentiles have tornados and floods, Jews have pogroms and anti-Semites. That's just the way it is.

(gets up to leave.)

JONATHAN: Going so soon? Someone get him an aerosol can of cheese.
SCHMELVIS: I think I'm allergic to the Rabbi. What kind of rabbi is he, making fun of Judaism like that? He should be ashamed.
JONATHAN: Come on, Schmel. He's a spiritual leader. He's just got a sense of humour. You're supposed to love your fellow Jews. Besides, he gave you sardines.
SCHMELVIS: Yeah, that's another way to say he gave me heartburn. I love the guy...as long as he's 3,000 miles away. I love him. Just keep him away from me.

We set out to find the lost grave of Elvis's great-great-grandmother Nancy Burdine Tackett, his last practising Jewish ancestor. She died in 1870. If the grave had a Star of David, it would have been definitive proof that Elvis was Jewish.

A search of six different graveyards turned up nothing. It was 108 degrees outside.

If those cheap bastards had forked out the money, the private investigator could have found her grave in an hour and we wouldn't have wasted half a day tramping through snake-infested boneyards on a wild Jew chase.

Schmelvis on the phone with his wife

Here in the South, they bury the Jews alongside the gentiles. It's not the way things are done. It's not right.

They have no sense of our traditions, our people's ways. The whole place is one big . . . one big . . . porkchop barbecue!

What the Winnebago smells like:

EVAN: Burning plastic and mold
MAX: Apples and hemorrhoids
SCHMELVIS: Raw pork and ear wax
MILA: Halitosis
JONATHAN: New car smell and intestines
DAN: Cat urine, eggs, and a hint of feces
ARI: Cheetos (which I don't mind) and feet (which I do mind)

Evan calls Auntie Pearlie at a payphone

EVAN: I just wanted to let you know how your investment is going.
PEARLIE: What are you doing with my money? Are you having a party with my money while I'm sitting at home eating consommé? Are you entertaining whores with my gelt? Is my nephew a mongerer of whores?
EVAN: But Auntie Pearlie, I have given the greatest gift of all, for chrissakes, the gift of immortality.

Why I became a vegan

by Evan Beloff

In 1986, I first noticed that my Greek neighbors were slaughtering farm animals in our backyard. It was Easter and they had dug a hole in the yard and were roasting this huge skinned lamb and it scared the shit out of me. I went over to my Russian *bubbe* (who had absolutely no sympathy for me) and asked for an explanation. She didn't have much to say. I realized years later she was boiling a two-pound cow's tongue as we talked. Come to think of it, every time I came to her to complain about the neighbors she was boiling a tongue of some kind. Ya know, Jewish cuisine, especially European Jewish cuisine, is based on a dare—chullent, schmaltz, tongue, barbecued fat, clear bone marrow, Jell-O. All Russian. All terrible. No wonder there's so much assimilation.

So I began to seriously consider my eating habits and then one day my mother asked me to defrost some lambchops and I realized as I looked over at these clean cuts neatly wrapped in cellophane—prime roast meat—that it was the most soulless thing ever, that I was a cannibal. I was always sensitive to animals. I once threw my arms around a horse that was being whipped by its owner in Old Montreal and would cry when I went to the butcher with my *bubbe* as a boy. But this was enough. I could not eat my friends anymore.

Jonathan's Journal

A Winnebago inhabited by seven men on the road for several days straight very quickly becomes Jonestown on wheels. When the crew picked me up, that Winnebago was a place you could eat off the floors. But after just a few days, it became infested with fruit flies. I may have even seen a cockroach. There were watermelon rinds and chip bags clogging the sink, the sun roof was smashed from going through a low tollbooth, and every time the RV took a wide turn, all the cutlery drawers would fly out and smash against the wall. After a while, we got tired of picking up all the spoons and forks and just left them there on the floor, relying on our fingers to eat the microwavable dinners that packed the RV freezer.

Jonathan's notes towards a novel he will never finish

Looking for Jerusalem, Alabama

Max gets it into his head that it'll be highly ironic if we all hang out in Jerusalem, Alabama. He thinks that's the best place to try to recruit our *minyan* of ten Jewish men. Get it? It's Jerusalem, the holy city, but it's also in the South. The thing is, he read this article in the *Jerusalem Post* about this all-black town called Jerusalem where none of the residents know there's another city in the world called Jerusalem.

He thinks it'll be hysterical to arrive there looking for Jews, only to find that everybody's black. He hasn't told any of the others on the Winnebago about what to expect when we get there. We spend five fucking hours riding around looking for the place. Everyone wants to kill each other. Max makes us pass a goddam football around in the back like we're all having the time of our lives.

Jerusalem, Alabama doesn't exist on any map! It doesn't exist, period. This whole thing started as an adventure and then it became a Beckett play.

So the Rabbi consults the Global Positioning Satellite Emergency System from his Cadillac. They direct us to the alleged location. After driving in the opposite direction another hour, we arrive at a deserted dead end called Palestine Road. At the end of the road is the Palestine Baptist Church.

"We set out looking for Jerusalem and we end up finding Palestine! That's rich. Oh God, that's good. That is beautiful," says the Rabbi.

BACK OF THE WINNEBAGO, OVERHEAD BED

Jonathan and Evan are lounging on the bed.

JONATHAN: In every relationship between two people, one guy ends up the Stimpy and one guy ends up the Ren. In your relationship with Ari, who do you think is who?

EVAN: You're setting me up here. Ari looks more like Stimpy.

JONATHAN: And . . .

EVAN: Okay, I'm the Ren. I'm the one with the throbbing stress vein and the pop-out marshmallow eyes. You happy? That what you want to hear?

JONATHAN: Does it bug you that you're the one who's always being labeled the bad guy?

EVAN: Who calls me a bad guy?

JONATHAN: No one.

EVAN: Bastard.

JONATHAN: You know what I mean.

EVAN: Look, Ari's such a nice guy because he doesn't know better. I have to look after the boy, or we'd all end up dead. I'm the guy who takes the flak and I'm prepared for that. It's just the way I'm built. I can weather the gut punches. It rolls off me.

JONATHAN: Really, I'm sure no one likes to have to shoulder the responsibility of being seen as the monster, the ogre, the grotesque of human evil.

EVAN: Do you think of me that way?

JONATHAN: Forty percent of the time.

EVAN: And the other sixty?

JONATHAN: Is sort of like theater of the absurd.

EVAN: That's what I am to you?

JONATHAN: You'd sell me down the river for the last slice of pizza on the plate.

EVAN: Do you really think that?

Why doesn't Ari start yelling at people? He's a producer here, too. How come I always have to look like the bad guy? Someone's got to get the job done. He acts like he's trying to win a popularity contest.

I'm losing money as I breathe and fart. We have to turn up something within the week or I'm dead.

Ari says, "Come on man. We're a bunch of characters. Just us being out here hanging around is going to be entertaining."

Fuck, Ari. You can't have a two-hour film of people just hanging around. I feel like I'm alone in this, that I'm the only one who cares. Everybody thinks this whole thing is a big joke.

What would each of your Spice Girls names be?

ARI: Moroccan spice

DAN: Get-out-of-my-face spice

EVAN: Classy spice

MAX: Show-me-the-money spice

JONATHAN: Embittered spice

MILA: I-wanna-go-home spice

SCHMELVIS: Paprika

Since you're suddenly the immortal bard, Ar, I thought I'd write you a poem:

Sing a song of friendship!
Musky male friendship! Of farts and sex stories!
O me, what a fool's fool I've been. I pound my foolhardy head
with the heel of my hand for the feel of retribution.
Of what use?
I cannot pound a ditch into this thickheaded bullshit factory
and so I weep.

What's that, gentle sparrow?
Weep not?
But why?
I am a loathsome foul blackguard
to have been so evil to a friend so dear
surely I am only worthy to sup with worms and the unemployable.
I have fallen from the dining table atop Mount Olympus
where I dined with the Gods —who know not of mortal problems
pettiness, various odors and the like
and now I am alone dear little sparrow,
so indeed don't go telling me I should not
(for this really isn't your business)
when weep I must!

What's that beaked friend?
I musn't fret because a friend like Ari will understand?

Well, why didn't you say so, sparrow?

From Elvis' Kitchen

PEANUT BUTTER &
BANANA SANDWICHES

2	large bananas
6	slices white bread
1	stick (1/2 cup) butter
1	cup peanut butter

Peel and mash bananas. Mix peanut butter with bananas thoroughly. Toast bread lightly and spread mix on bread. Melt butter in skillet and brown sandwiches on each side slowly until golden brown.

Elvis's Favorite Meal

Fried Peanut Butter & Banana Sandwich

This is reported to be the recipe that Gladys (Elvis's mom) used:

2 tablespoons smooth peanut butter
2 slices white bread
2 tablespoons margarine
1 ripe banana

Spread peanut butter extra thick between slices of bread. Melt margarine in frying pan over medium heat. Brown sandwich on both sides in melted margarine.

As sandwich browns, mash banana in a bowl. Remove browned sandwich from pan, gingerly pry open, and spread mashed banana on warm peanut butter.

Serve immediately while still warm. Eat with knife and fork.

Serve with an 8 oz. glass of milk.

Schmelvis's Favorite Meal

Yoina Schimmel's Potato Kugel
(Potato Pudding)
8 servings
3 lbs Idaho potatoes
1/8 teaspoon pepper
4 eggs
1/4 cup grated onion
1/3 cup potato flour
1/2 cup butter, melted
1 1/2 teaspoon salt
3/4 teaspoon baking powder

Wash and peel the potatoes. Coarsely grate the potatoes into a large bowl filled with ice water. Let stand for at least 15 minutes.

Preheat the oven to 350° F. Grease the inside of a 1 1/2 quart baking dish.

Drain the potatoes. Pat dry. You'll need about 5 1/2 cups of grated potatoes for 8 servings (adjust as required).

Use the large bowl of an electric mixer running at high speed to beat the eggs until they are thick and light. Stir in the potatoes, potato flour, salt, baking powder, pepper, onions, and half the melted butter.

Mix well. Turn into the prepared baking dish.

Bake, uncovered, for 30 minutes, brushing the top with melted butter every 10 minutes until it top is crusty and golden brown.

90

The kitchen table in the Winnebago turns into a bed. That is the foul magic of the Winnebago right there. These are things that should only happen in dreams. Nightmares, perhaps. Where the bed that Schmelvis sleeps should become the place you eat bacon and eggs on every morning. This Winnebago is a testimony to the ever-shape-shifting, amorphous aspect of human reality. Try and sanctify something. I just dare you.

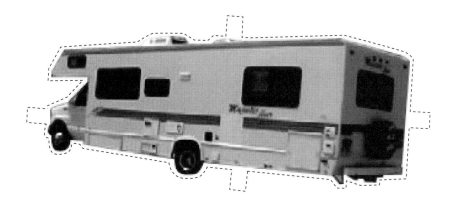

MEMPHIS, LANSKY'S TAILOR SHOP.

Jonathan interviews BERNARD LANSKY, "Clothier to the King," in a store sporting guitars that onced belonged to Elvis hanging from the ceiling and sparkly satin outfits.

LANSKY: I put his first suit on him and his last suit. I made him sharp, clean as Ajax. You know what Ajax is? It keeps you clean. He was sharp. I made him look good.
JONATHAN: How?

LANSKY: Without someone making the clothes, all you've got is a big fat naked boy. Understand? If we were all naked, there would be no variety. All there'd be is "that cat's dong is longer than my dong. That kid's peter is fatter than my peter."And that gets old real fast, so when you got someone sewing slacks, then you've got something to make things interesting. It's like the curtains before the play. Without the curtains, all you've got is people running around on a stage, nothing to tell you that what you're about to see is in any way special. Without the pants, all you got is a bunch of shrivelled dongs looking to party. I'm old, but I ain't that old. I understand that there gotta be some glaze on the doughnut to make the doughnut look good. Understand? Of course you do. You ain't no dummy.

JONATHAN: Of course I'm not. But for the sake of argument, let's suppose that I am. Let's imagine that I'm so dumb that I truly do not understand what you're trying to get across to me. So when you say this business about a doughnut, and trousers, what are you trying to actually say?

LANSKY: Alright, here's the dope. Say you went around showing off your willie all day. You think that willie would be special? Hell, it would be as special as the nose on your face. Ever see a lady sucking someone's nose in an alley for fifty beans? Course not, cause that'd be absurd. Correct? I'm saying that not only do the clothes make the man, they make the soul of the man, cause if you had to go around looking at a man's soul all day long, you would-n't be able to see it for all the dongs.

JONATHAN: I haven't a clue what you're trying to tell me.

LANSKY: The King always understood what I told him.

JONATHAN: That's why he was the King.

LANSKY: I guess that's so.

(*SCHMELVIS joins them.*)

SCHMELVIS: Did you know Elvis was Jewish?

LANSKY: Naw.

SCHMELVIS: He wore the Jewish *chai*.

LANSKY: Yeah, George Klein gave it to him.

SCHMELVIS: Who?

LANSKY: George Klein. He was Elvis's best buddy. He was in the Memphis Mafia, Elvis's entourage. He probably gave Elvis that *chai*.

SCHMELVIS: Yeah, but he also put a Star of David on his mother's headstone.

LANSKY: George Klein told him to do that. Anything that George Klein told him to do, Elvis would do.

THE UNIVERSITY OF MEMPHIS, AMPHITHEATER.

(*GEORGE KLEIN has just finished speaking at the Elvis Reunion, part of the Elvis Week festivities which has reunited the Memphis Mafia, the King's personal entourage.*)

SCHMELVIS (*approaching Klein*): Did Elvis ever say anything about being Jewish?

KLEIN: I know he had Jewish blood on his mother's side, his great-grandmother or something like that. And Elvis always wore a Jewish *chai*. I guess you have one on. I do too. He was actually wearing the Jewish *chai* when he died. He once had watches made with a flashing Star of David and crucifix and distributed them to all his friends.

SCHMELVIS: Do you know why he put a Star of David on his mother's headstone?

KLEIN: No, we never knew why he did that.

SCHMELVIS: When they moved Elvis's grave from Forest Hills to Graceland, do you know why they removed the Star of David?

KLEIN: The Star of David wasn't removed. The whole footstone was removed. There just wasn't enough room, I guess, up there in Graceland. They still have it in storage and I'm sure one day they'll bring it out.

Jonathan interviews two cleaning women about Evan's choice of hairstyle.

WOMAN #1: He looks like a Chinaman. He looks like a Chinaman working on the railroad.
WOMAN #2: He looks like he just got out of a Russian mental hospital, the poor thing. Look at him, all pink and blotchy.
JONATHAN: He's a vegan.
WOMAN #1: A what?
JONATHAN: He doesn't eat meat.
WOMAN #1: Then what's he eat?
JONATHAN: Not only does he not eat meat, he doesn't eat eggs or cheese or even the occasional Coca Cola.
WOMAN #2 (*laughing*): What's he live on? The sun?
JONATHAN: He eats vitamins and weird syrups all day. He's always dripping something from an eye dropper onto his tongue and making this face like he's about to gag.
WOMAN #2: He looks like Prince Valiant. Why would someone want to do something like that?
JONATHAN: He's always been like this. He breaks my heart.
WOMAN #2: Why don't you shave his head while he's sleeping?
JONATHAN: Don't you think I've tried it? He wakes up as nasty as a ferret being skinned alive. I'm worried that he won't find a bride at this rate.
WOMAN #1: Well, he's cute enough. He just has to get rid of that haircut. It's for a stooge, you know? Like Larry from the "Three Stooges."
JONATHAN: Will you speak to him? He won't listen to me.

(*The women walk away.*)

EVAN: Why do you do that to me?
JONATHAN: You love it. It's the only thing you understand.

Jonathan's Journal

Evan's got a Peter Pan complex. All those sit-ups and soy beverages. The poor bastard's scared of looking in the mirror and seeing his father one day. But it happens to all of us.

The crew sits in iron wrought chairs under towering palms drinking mint juleps.

JONATHAN: Max, I like movies as much as the next guy, but where is this film headed? Every film has to be about something. What's this film about? We came to Memphis expecting to be burned at the stake and suddenly everybody loves us. That doesn't exactly make for good cinema.

EVAN: What's wrong with a feel-good documentary?

JONATHAN: Now he thinks it's a feel-good documentary. Wow! Seriously, does anybody think it's important anymore if we find out Elvis is Jewish?

THE GROUP: No!

MAX: That's what we started out to find but it's obviously become much bigger than that.

SCHMELVIS: Who cares if Elvis is Jewish? Jonathan, are you Jewish?

JONATHAN: Am I supposed to answer that seriously?

RABBI: No, for once I agree with Schmelvis. Elvis didn't do anything about his Judaism. What are you doing about yours, Jon? Maybe Elvis represents every lost Jew in the melting pot of America.

JONATHAN (*visibly annoyed*): Maybe he doesn't. I haven't seen that at all.

They all argue.

DAN (the sound man):

These assholes don't know the first thing about film, but you know what? I couldn't care fucking less. I don't even want my name associated with this monstrosity. I start teaching film in Alberta next semester and in the meantime I can bring in a couple extra grand before I take off. It'll go a long way. I've got a wife and two kids and I've got to think of them. When I'm ready to strangle Max, that's all I have to think of. As far as anyone will ever know, Buddy Freejack was the soundman on this film. Let them ruin Buddy's career. Not mine.

MILA (the cameraman):

I've always wanted to see the South. Doing a shoot here is cool. Dan loses it. He says he doesn't care, but he loses it. At night I can hear him making strangling noises while he's sleeping. I look over at him and he's got spit coming out of the sides of his mouth. I guess I just like to travel and I like shooting stuff. If I was in a prison cell with a camera, I'd end up with hourglass-sand zooms and pans of the walls.

ARI (executive producer):

I don't know. It seemed like a pretty good idea, you know? Evan seemed really into it. It's nice to get a chance to hang out like this with everyone. It's cool to be making a movie like this. It beats the shit out of an office job or a factory job. And the best thing about travel is that you never have to feel guilty you ate three snickers bars for lunch or you didn't call someone back. You never have to feel bad that you didn't call someone back. There aren't as many chances to hurt someone on the road.

SCHMELVIS (the star):

Look, I have a high-stress job. The idea of taking to the road has a certain romance to it. I saw myself ripping off my necktie as I boarded the Winnebago, like that car commercial? If they're making jokes with me I don't mind; what I don't like is to be made a laughingstock. Who likes that? Even a jester had a place in the royal court. You see? I think this whole thing is the world of exile on wheels. But without me, there's no movie. Who's going to be the star? The Rabbi? Do they think they can make a movie with him? Or Max? Jonathan? Not only do you need an ass to fill out the Schmelvis suit, you also need a brain. You have to know what to put out, when to hold back, you know?

EVAN (producer):

I am the bad cop and Ari is the good cop, but what people don't realize is that without me there's nothing. You can't have Mr. Nice Guy running an office twenty-four on seven, so I get saddled with all the dirty work. I should probably get my head examined. I've got psychosomatic anal warts from stress. I got into it because I thought it might be a good way to make my mark, you know, "there's the guy who produced *Schmelvis*." But instead it's "there's the guy who bled his poor aunt for every ounce of her pension money. For shame!"

MAX (director):

I'm not what you'd call a film buff. The last movie I went to was the one about that guy who was retarded, *Forrest Gump*. I think I slept through most of it. I was dating a social worker at the time and I was going to make her happy. All I remember from the movie is her sitting beside me, tugging at my arm and saying, "Don't you feel sad for him?" We broke up pretty soon after that. What I mean to say is that I don't give a crap for the movies. Give me a big fat novel any day. Christ, I'd take the goddamn Bible over *Forrest Gump*. But in this case, a movie is the perfect medium. I don't know if you noticed, but these are a bunch of very visual guys.

JONATHAN (associate producer):

I feel like Alice to Evan's Ralph Kramden. Is Elvis Jewish? I could't give a shit and I honestly don't think these guys give a damn either. But we're all showmen in the great vaudeville tradition, and that's what we're here to do: Put on a show in the great tradition of the great late vaudevillians of years gone by. If you watch Schmelvis with the color turned down, in fast motion, you will see a man who owes more to Fatty Arbuckle than to Elvis Presley.

REUBEN POUPKO (the rabbi):

You call this a documentary, an investigation? Investigating means going to libraries, doing research, poring through archives, city records. We drive around in circles in a Winnebago and a Cadillac like idiots. That's not investigating. That's what children do. You think you can come down here and unlock the mysteries of the South? The South holds her secrets.

16 GRACELAND, FRONT GATES. EVENING.

*On the eve of the 23rd anniversary of Elvis's death, August 16,
2000, thousands of people gather to commemorate the event at the
annual candlelight vigil.*

*Schmelvis is decked out in his white polyester jumpsuit complete
with decorative Stars of David and a red satin cape. He also wears
a big chai.*

*Evan and Schmelvis interview a woman who has a T-shirt bearing the
inscription "I knew Elvis."*

EVAN: You knew the King?
WOMAN: When I was fifteen, I was living in this little town in
Texas — Palesteen — and Elvis came through in his Cadillac and asked
me for directions to a gas station. I directed him to my cousin's
filling station down the road. Then almost twenty years later, I
went to see him in concert and I told him the story and he remembered me. He never forgot a face, you know.
SCHMELVIS: I'm sure Elvis never forgot a pretty face.
WOMAN (*blushing and punching Schmelvis on the shoulder*): Thank
you.

(*Schmelvis smiles and makes an exit.*)

EVAN: Can I ask you a couple of questions?
WOMAN: Sure.
EVAN: Did Elvis ever discuss with you his spiritual side?
WOMAN: No, we never got into that kind of a conversation.
EVAN: Well, we discovered through research that Elvis was a Jew.
Did you know that?
WOMAN: I knew Gladys went back that way.
EVAN: You knew that? How did you know that?
WOMAN: Books and such.
EVAN: Why do you think he never discussed it?
WOMAN: It wasn't important enough to discuss.
EVAN: He discussed a million times that he was a Baptist.
WOMAN: Elvis was never a Baptist.
EVAN: He wasn't a Baptist?
WOMAN: He belonged to the Assembly of God.
EVAN: Well, he must have thought it was important. He wore a Star
of David around his neck.

WOMAN: He said he didn't want to get left out of heaven on a technicality.

EVAN: Well, if that was true, he would have worn medallions from the 700 different religions in the world.

WOMAN: He did.

EVAN: Why do you think it wasn't important enough to discuss?

WOMAN: Jewish people might be interested. But the average Elvis fan like me couldn't care less.

EVAN: I don't have an agenda or anything. I'm just here with my man Schmelvis taking in the scene. Have you met Schmelvis?

WOMAN: Yeah, I've met SMELLvis.

EVAN: Not SMELLvis. SCHMELLvis.

WOMAN: You say that different.

EVAN: SCHMELLvis.

WOMAN: Sh-sh-sh-SCHMELLvis.

EVAN: Now you've got it.

SCHMELVIS (*to the Rabbi*): Why do you think he's pulling so many people in?

RABBI: He's a martyr, a martyred hero. He comforts them when they're lonely, a woman told me. It's paganism.

GRACELAND, FRONT GATES

(*Schmelvis corners a WOMAN.*)

SCHMELVIS: You say he wasn't a Jew. I want to know why.
WOMAN: Because he was a Christian. He's in heaven now because once you are saved, you will always be saved.
SCHMELVIS: I'm not saying he was a practising Jew. He ate bacon more than anybody in this crowd. But his mother was Jewish and that makes him Jewish.
WOMAN: Nonsense. He wasn't a Jew.
SCHMELVIS: How do you know?
WOMAN: Because I used to guard him. I have nothing against Jews. My godfather is the number one supporter of the State of Israel.
SCHMELVIS: Elvis?
WOMAN: No, Doctor Jerry Falwell.

(*The RABBI joins them.*)

RABBI: Tell me something. What percentage of the United States do you think is Jewish?
WOMAN: I'd say 38 percent, between 38-40 percent.
RABBI: Actually, it's less than 2 percent.
WOMAN: Who says so?
RABBI: The census. The U.S. census. Do you think it's a lie?
WOMAN: Yeah, I think it's a lie.
RABBI: What do you think it is?
WOMAN: 38 percent.

(*She goes off to find a SECURITY GUARD.*)

WOMAN: They're making trouble. They're claiming Elvis wasn't a Christian.

(*Everywhere SCHMELVIS goes, young women swarm around him and ask him to pose for photos. ARI & EVAN watch from a distance.*)

ARI: Look at Schmelvis. All those beautiful women surrounding him. I feel like stealing his costume and putting it on myself. I'd go to Mardi Gras and all the big parades. I'd go up to women and pinch their ass, say, "Look at me, I'm Elvis."
EVAN: Like a sexual predator in a costume?
ARI: You're damn right. Look at those women. They're beautiful.

Schmelvis calls his wife

To be honest, I wasn't too crazy about all of the attention. They were loving me, but I was schvitzing like a dog and I just wanted to get home and take a shower.

I would have liked to just walk around looking at all the weirdos and the freaks but I couldn't because I was the weirdo and the freak.

We ran into an Elvis impersonator at the vigil who knew a lot about Elvis's Jewish roots. He said he was a good friend of Larry Geller, Elvis's spiritual adviser, who told him the inside story.

He said that Elvis's father Vernon didn't want anybody to know that Gladys and Elvis were Jewish so he removed the Star of David from her headstone. He says that he was with Elvis when he originally decided to put the Star of David on the headstone many years after Gladys actually died. Originally, there was just a crucifix on it. He said Elvis told him that his mother Gladys had taken him aside when he was young and told him that they had Jewish blood but that he shouldn't talk about it because a lot of people didn't like Jews back then.

Jonathan's Journal

"What is it about Elvis that so blows your mind?" I asked one woman from Kansas. She comes to Graceland every August.

"He reminds me of when I was a teenager. He makes me feel young."

I wonder if that's how Jesus started out, twenty years after his death—merely making his disciples feel young.

From what I've gathered talking to Schmelvis, Chassidic Jews are biding their time waiting for the Messiah to come and lead them to the Holy Land where they'll live in peace in harmony. Now we get to Memphis and discover that all these Elvis fanatics seem to have turned the King into their own Messiah. I keep wondering if there's a connection. Maybe that's why Schmelvis says he's always had a spiritual connection to Elvis Presley.

At the vigil, there was this guy handing out pamphlets for something called the "First Presleytarian Church of Elvis the Divine." Sure enough, it confirms everything we've observed. None of us can figure out if they're serious. None of these people we meet seem to have any sense of irony about their Elvis worship. Memphis seems to be a place where irony goes to die.

Doctrine of the First Presleytarian Church of Elvis the Divine

THE KING'S PRAYER

Our Elvis who art not in heaven but here among us now;
Thy will be done, thy kingdom come, in Tupelo as it is in Memphis.
Give us this day our daily song and
forgive those who understand not the King's power.
They know not what they do.
For thine is the Kingdom, the power and the Graceland.
Forever and ever.
Amen.

For those who knew Him best, He would be described
well in "The Letter to The Hebrews."

His own identity is best understood in "Isaiah."

His life on Earth is theologically baffling to many!

He had twelve men on His pay-roll who did serve as
"body-guards"; and They were His closest companions
for the large portion of His adult life.

He enjoyed the company of a woman, who some thought of
as being a "fallen woman." However, this did not prevent
them from having a very amicable friendship.

Biblically, she is referred to as "Mary of Magdalene."

His generation was "The Jesus Freak Generation"
which is scripturally concise when We study the
textual facts of "Isaiah" and His life.

In "Isaiah," The Lord proclaims that He has formed
Them [His followers] with His lips; and made Them
with His words. This is precise when One considers
how The Messiah would accomplish His mission
in a world that runs on economics.

The Messiah must make large sums of money to fulfill
His destiny; yet He must not be restrained by
subjection to the day-to-day demands of worldly
concerns as so many have had to surrender too.

i.e. (9 to 5, dusk to dawn)
(paycheck to paycheck and still broke)
(no clout - no doubt - get out)
World We live in.

He was born in accord with the astrological sign of Capricorn.

He was born in the winter soltice.

The town He was born in had no notoriety.

His family later moved, not ever moving back.

The world knew Him NOT as The Messiah.

He has followers who confess Him as The Messiah, and they have done so openly.

He did teach His Apostles in the upper room of Graceland.

Jesus vs. Elvis

Besides their common Jewish heritage, Elvis Presley, the "King of Rock," had much in common with Jesus Christ, the "King of all Kings":

1. Jesus said, "Love thy neighbor" (Matthew 22:39).

   Elvis said, "Don't Be Cruel" (RCA, 1956).

2. Jesus H. Christ has 12 letters.

   Elvis Presley has 12 letters.

3. Jesus is the Lord's shepherd.

   Elvis dated Cybill Shepherd.

4. Jesus said, "Man shall not live by bread alone" (Matthew 4:4).

   Elvis loved his sandwiches with peanut butter and bananas.

5. "Then they took up stones to cast at [Jesus]" (John 8:59).

   Elvis was often stoned.

6. Jesus was the Lamb of God.

   Elvis had mutton chops.

7. Jesus was part of a Trinity.

   Elvis's first band was a trio.

8. Jesus walked on water (Matthew 14:25).

   Elvis surfed (*Blue Hawaii*, Paramount, 1965).

9. Jesus was a carpenter.

   Elvis majored in woodshop/industrial arts in high school.

10. Jesus lived in a state of grace in a Near Eastern land.

    Elvis lived in Graceland in a nearly eastern state.

11. Jesus wore the crown of thorns.

    Elvis wore Royal Crown hair styler.

12. Jesus' entourage, the Apostles, had 12 members.

    Elvis's entourage, the Memphis Mafia, had 12 members.

13. A major woman in Jesus' life (Mary) had an immaculate conception.

    A major woman in Elvis's life (Priscilla) went to Immaculate Conception high school.

14. Jesus was resurrected.

    Elvis had the famous comeback special in 1968.

15. Son of God.	Sun Studios.
16. Jesus said, "If any man thirst, let him come unto me, and drink" (John 7:37).	Elvis said, "Drinks on me!" (*Jailhouse Rock*, MGM, 1957).
17. Jesus fasted for 40 days and nights.	Elvis had irregular eating habits (e.g., five banana splits for breakfast).
18. Jesus is a Capricorn (Dec. 25).	Elvis is a Capricorn (Jan. 8).
19. Jesus biography by Matthew (Gospel according to Matthew).	Elvis biography by Neal Matthews (*Elvis: A Golden Tribute*).
20. "[Jesus'] countenance was like lightning, and his raiment white as snow" (Matthew 28:3).	Elvis' trademarks were a lightning bolt and snow-white jumpsuits.
21. There is much confusion about Jesus' middle name—what does the "H" stand for?	There is much confusion about Elvis' middle name—was it Aron or Aaron?
22. Jesus made rocks roll away from his tomb.	Elvis was a rock and roll singer.

We heard that Elvis grew up in Memphis's Jewish neighborhood, the Pinch, and that, when he was a teenager, he lived downstairs from a local rabbi, Alfred Fruchter. So we head to the Pinch to scout for Jewish old-timers who might have known the young Elvis. We locate the Rabbi's widow, Jeannette Fruchter, who is still alive. We pay her a visit.

MRS. FRUCHTER: My husband was the rabbi of a large Orthodox synagogue in Memphis and we were living upstairs in a two-storey house on 150 Alabama Ave. One day the downsatirs apartment became vacant. The Presleys were living in low-income housing at Lauderdale Courts but the father, Vernon, got a job and all of a sudden they were making too much money for low-income housing. It must have been his mother, Gladys, who came by and saw the apartment for rent. The next week, they moved in.

MAX: How old was Elvis at the time?

MRS. FRUCHTER: He was about 15 years old then and we got along so beautifully. He was such a nice boy, such manners. He called my husband "Sir Rabbi." Gladys came over every afternoon for tea and cake and we would talk. She wanted Elvis to be a doctor but he wasn't such an excellent student. I told her, 'Gladys, don't push him. You'll see, one day he'll make you happy. Give him time.'

MAX: There's a rumor that Elvis used to be your *Shabbos Goy*. Any truth to that?

MRS. FRUCHTER: Orthodox Jews are not allowed to use electricity or make phone calls on the Sabbath. So Elvis would come over every Saturday morning, every Sabbath, and he would turn the lights on and do other things for us. We never told him we called him a *Shabbos Goy*, we didn't mean any harm by it. Usually, you give a small tip to the gentile who does this for you. They were very poor. But Elvis would never accept any money, he said it was his pleasure.

MAX: Did they ever come over for Sabbath dinner?

MRS. FRUCHTER: Once a month, we would have them over for Friday night dinner. Elvis loved our food, especially the challah. I heard later on he would have his peanut butter and banana sandwiches on challah. He loved matzo ball soup and chimmes.

MAX: Did Elvis wear a *yarmulke*?

MRS. FRUCHTER: He always carried a *yarmulke* in his pocket.

MAX: Did you know he had Jewish blood?

MRS. FRUCHTER: We didn't know then but I heard there's a Star of David on his headstone.

MAX: He put one on his mother's footstone.

MRS. FRUCHTER: Yes, on his mother's. But also on his, I think. I don't know. I never saw it but that's what I heard.

MAX: Did Elvis ever listen to Jewish music when he visited you?

MRS. FRUCHTER: My husband used to love Jewish cantorial music. He listened to all the greats, Rubinstein, Moishe Oishe. It was very hot in Memphis in the summertime and we always had the windows open. So the music would drift up to Elvis's apartment and he would hear it. He told us that he loved listening to it. Some people think it may have influenced his own style, they've heard a Jewish twist to some of his tunes. I don't know.

I remember when he cut his first record for his mother's birthday. He had paid a couple of dollars at the Sun music studio. When he got home with it, they couldn't play it because they were too poor to afford a record player. So my husband lent him ours. He was so thankful. They would play that first song over and over again. That's what started his career, you know, that recording.

MAX: Did you ever keep in touch after he became famous?

MRS. FRUCHTER: No, we didn't see him very often. But we heard about how he would give money to Jewish charities quite often and we thought maybe it was because he remembered us. We didn't know that he might be Jewish, of course.

MAX: He gave money to Jewish causes?

MRS. FRUCHTER: Oh yes. One day the Memphis Jewish Welfare sent a delegation to Graceland to ask if he could contribute something. At Christmas every year he would donate $1,000 to a number of Memphis charities and one of them was the Memphis Hebrew Academy, and so they thought maybe they could get something. They explained what they do, taking care of poor Jews, orphans and such, and he excused himself for a minute. When he came back, he handed the leader of the delegation a check. They didn't know what to expect. They thought $1,000 would be nice. When they looked at the check, it was for $150,000. That's the equivalent of more than a million dollars today.

The man said, 'Elvis, you must have made a mistake.' Elvis said, 'I didn't make a mistake, I know what I'm doing.' Later on, he also donated a room to the old Memphis Jewish Community Center.

Mrs. Fruchter tells us we should interview the Presleys' old landlady, Fagie Shaffer, who lives in a suburb of Memphis. We call her up and arrange a visit.

Fagie Schaffer

MRS. SHAFFER: Elvis used to come by once a month to deliver their rent check, I think they paid $50. He was a very nice boy. My mother used to call him *Elvis'l*, which is a Yiddish term of endearment.
SCHMELVIS: What do you remember about him?
MRS. SHAFFER (leafing through her old scrapbook of photos and articles about Elvis): When I first knew him, he had a big nose and not such a beautiful skin. But after his surgery, he turned into a very fine looking young man.
SCHMELVIS: What kind of surgery?
MRS. SHAFFER: Nose surgery.

(Pause)

MAX: Are you saying that Elvis had a nose job?
MRS. SHAFFER: Yes I am. You don't believe me (*finds a photo of young Elvis from the scrapbook*). Look, here's his original nose.

After the interview, the group leaves her apartment to board the Winnebago.

MAX: Today we learned that Elvis's mother wanted him to be a doctor; he loved matzo ball soup, and he had a nose job. If that doesn't prove that he's Jewish, nothing will. What more proof do we need?

Graceland, August 16, 2000
The 23rd Anniversary of Elvis's death

Rabbi Poupko: This is guerrilla warfare on a spiritual level. We're going to claim a lost Jewish soul. We're going to say *kaddish* for Elvis Presley, Elvis AARON Presley, I might add. We say *kaddish* to elevate someone's soul to God. Nobody ever said *kaddish* for Elvis Presley. We're going to give him the Jewish consecration he deserves.

Schmelvis: I wish Elvis was alive right now. I'd wrap *tfillin* on the guy. I'd say to him. "Elvis, you know what it is to be a Jew? Did you eat kosher today? Did you say your *shmas*?" Those are the important things. He had a wonderland toyland in his backyard and he got tired of all his toys. That's why he's not here today. He got tired of life.

Jonathan: Graceland. I don't know what I was expecting. It seems too small somehow. The inside of the house is the height of 70's chic. It's dimly lit with a lot of browns and corduroy and carpeted walls. The kitchen is even carpeted. It's got a pinball machine and a pool table. It's the kind of house a little boy would decorate for himself. I was kind of disappointed by the TV room. It had three TVs side by side which Elvis would watch at the same time tuned to three different channels, but they all had their screens intact. If they wanted to go for authenticity, a couple of the screens would be shot out because that's what Elvis would do whenever he was pissed off with something he was watching. Now that's cultural commentary the way it should be done.

Max: While on the tour, we run into Elvis's old cook, an old black woman who somebody tells us is called Brown Mama. I ask her if it's true that Elvis ate his peanut butter and banana sandwiches slathered in pork grease. She confirms it. But she says he never allowed shellfish in the house, which is one of the kosher dietary prohibitions. Maybe he just didn't know enough about Judaism to know that pork was also on the taboo list. I pressed the issue and asked if Elvis liked chicken soup. Brown Mama shared her recipe, which she said Elvis loved, but it contained tomatoes. That's not the way my *bubbe* made it.

The highlight of the tour was seeing Elvis's Jewish *chai* displayed in a glass case. There's no mention of Judaism, just a little note about how Elvis was interested in all religions. There were a couple of other Jewish symbols displayed as well, including a cabalistic pendant. We were all impressed.

Brown Mama's Chicken Soup

Makes about six bowls

5-6 lb chicken (a big, fat one), cut up
1 medium onion, peeled and quartered
1 large carrot, peeled, cut in two chunks
1 large celery stalk, cut in two chunks
2 ripe tomatoes, peeled, seeded, and chopped
1 bay leaf
1 1/2 teaspoon salt
1/2 teaspoon pepper

Place all of the ingredients in a stock pot and cover with water, about 8 cups. Cover and bring to a boil. Simmer for 1 hour. Uncover and simmer for 45 minutes, until the chicken is tender but not falling off the bones.

Let stand until cool. Strain the soup into a large bowl. Mash the onion and return it to the stock. Cut vegetables into bite-sized pieces. Remove meat from chicken and tear into bite-sized pieces. Add to the stock.

Kaddish

English Translation

RABBI: *Yis'ga'dal v'yis'kadash sh'may ra'bbo, b'olmo dee'vro chir'usay v'yamlich malchu'say, b'chayaychon uv'yomay'chon uv'chayay d'chol bais Yisroel, ba'agolo u'viz'man koriv; v'imru*
GROUP: *Omein.*
RABBI: *Y'hay shmay rabbo m'vorach l'olam ul'olmay olmayo. Yisborach àv'yishtabach v'yispoar v'yisromam v'yismasay, v'yishador v'yis'aleh v'yisalal, shmay d'kudsho, brich hu, l'aylo min kl birchoso v'sheeroso, tush'bechoso v'nechemoso, da,ameeran b'olmo; vimru*
GROUP: *Omein.*
RABBI: *Y'hay shlomo rabbo min sh'mayo, v'chayim alaynu v'al kol Yisroel; v'imru*
GROUP: *Omein.*
RABBI: *Oseh sholom bimromov, hu ya'aseh sholom olaynu, v'al kol yisroel; vimru*
GROUP: *Omein.*

May the great Name of God be exalted and sanctified, throughout the world, which he has created according to his will. May his Kingship be established in your lifetime and in your days, and in the lifetime of the entire household of Israel, swiftly and in the near future; and say, Amen.

May his great name be blessed, forever and ever. Blessed, praised, glorified, exalted, extolled, honored elevated and lauded be the Name of the holy one, Blessed is he - above and beyond any blessings and hymns, Praises and consolations which are uttered in the world; and say Amen. May there be abundant peace from Heaven, and life, upon us and upon all Israel; and say, Amen. He who makes peace in his high holy places, may he bring peace upon us, and upon all Israel; and say Amen.

Schmelvis on the phone to his wife

How's the trip? How's the trip? I'm ready to shove a confederate flag up my ass and start playing Dixie on a bagpipe. Do you know what I just did, Debbie? I turned the prayer for the dead into an episode of *Survivor*. I've blasphemed. I'm blaspheming all over the place. I just told the Rabbi he has his head up his ass. This to a rabbi! He's not a rabbi . . . he's a . . . I don't know what he is, but he's certainly not a teacher, the sick bastard—listen to me, will you. I just said *kaddish* for Elvis Presley. . . . That's right. Well, that was the whole point of the trip, wasn't it? I think I'm going to throw up. There was a goddam Chicano boy in our *minyan*. No I'm not joking. Max said Esperanto was close enough to Sephardim. I'm nauseous. I know. . . . Yes I thought Presley was Jewish, but this! Graceland! It's a circus, not a cemetery. I don't even know anymore. I'm going to *Gehenna* for sure. I'm calling Rabbi Fine. I have to gargle. My God, I wish I was home. . . . Why did you agree to this? Why did you agree to let me do this?

Director's Log, Aug. 16, 2000 — Research Notes

Elvis impersonators don't like being called "Elvis impersonators." They like to be called "Elvis tribute artists."

At Graceland, a three-hundred pound Elvis tribute artist named J.R. is on stage singing "Pork Salad Annie" while his manager hobbles around on crutches handing out business cards: "Ideal for bachelorette parties." J.R. keeps stopping in the middle of the song to drink from the largest plastic cup I have ever seen. Every time he puts the straw to his lips, I click my camera, but I can't seem to time it right. I have this beautiful photo in mind of a big Elvis and a big beverage coming together perfectly, but I just can't seem to get it right.

At Graceland, I go into the diner and ask for a fried peanut butter and banana sandwich in honor of Elvis. The woman behind the counter tells me that they're out of white bread.

"Then can you make it for me on one of the hamburger buns?" I ask, trying to keep my shit together.

She looks at me with her lip turned up slightly at the corner, like I've just made some terrible faux pas.

Lady, I'm thinking, I'm eating the anthemic treat of the fat pompadoured bastard who probably died on the shitter with a basket of the things on his lap and

you're looking at me like I just asked for the steak tartar well done. I'm eating a sandwich literally saturated in pig fat, swimming in lard, bubbling in hog sweat, and I don't think we should be mincing over what's going to be bookending the artery-clogging, cardiac-arresting peanut buttered hemlock. I don't care if it's slapped together with Styrofoam, bibles, newspaper . . . I'd eat it smooshed between a pair of tattered and stinky sneakers. I'm in Graceland and I want to live a little.

She brings it back to me and it's on white bread.

"I found some in the back."

Imagine that. Imagine the headlines: "White bread found at Graceland."

Jonathan's Journal

They want to shoot a scene of me and Evan on the roof of the Winnebago. I think that that'll be nice. Us up there on the Winnebago, shooting the shit, the Elvis Heartbreak Hotel in the background, drinking beer, talking against the Memphis sky as the sun is going down.

I have to get on the hood of the car and somehow will my body onto the roof. I put my hands on the roof and try to lift myself up. Mila and Dan are already up there. It's like they floated onto the roof on Hong Kong action picture wires. Evan and I stand on the hood of the Winnebago, our eyes looking at their feet. They come over and pull us up like the sacks of crap that we are —Evan a slightly heavier sack of crap than I am.

Jonathan interviews a WOMAN with an Elvis tattoo on her leg.

JONATHAN: That's a very life-like tattoo you have there.
WOMAN: Thank-you.
JONATHAN: It looks like it could just walk right off your leg and start singing.
WOMAN: Well, it was done by an expert.
JONATHAN: No prison tattoo for you, huh?
WOMAN: No sir.
JONATHAN: Do you ever have days when you wish you just didn't have that thing?
WOMAN: Never.
JONATHAN: Never?
WOMAN: Haven't you ever really loved someone?
JONATHAN: Yeah, but having them on my leg would freak me out.
WOMAN: This way, I always feel he's with me.
JONATHAN: Why not just a framed photo on the wall?
WOMAN: Well, then I'd never be able to leave the house.

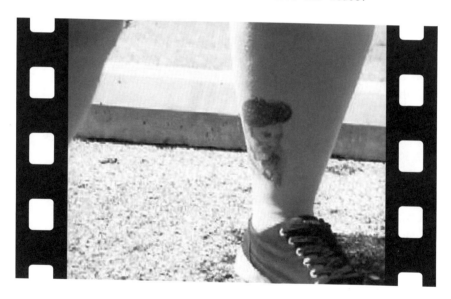

Evan's Production Journal

Everyone's always going on about what a goddam class act Elvis was, how he'd show up at the doorstep of some poor black blues singer he ripped off and present him with a big red Cadillac.

"What an A-1 class act," people say when they learn about such acts of seemingly gratuitous generosity.

"What a gentleman. A classy sort," these same misguided souls cry out from the confusion and darkness that is their lives. For them, Elvis is the flickering candle of class in a world of punk rock and chaos theory.

"Elvis loves us all," some poor creature told me outside the gates of Graceland on the first night of Elvis Week. "If he's looking down on all of this, which I'm sure he is."

"How can you know this for sure?" I ask.

The woman turns to me and speaks these next words as though addressing an idiot.

"What kind of a God wouldn't let Elvis see all the love that's being expressed to him down here? There isn't a question in my mind about whether Elvis is seeing all this."

What Elvis would in fact be seeing are tragically obese figures—the average Elvis fan—sitting on lawn chairs, holding candles, a hundred odd Elvis buttons stapled to their stomach and chest.

"Do you think he sees us right now?" I ask.

"He might. He might be scanning the crowd and his eye might have caught upon us."

"Is there anything you'd want to say to him if he is with us right now?"

"Well, Elvis, I love you and miss you and I just want you to know that you're still as important to us as you ever were."

"Is he as important to you as your children are?"

"In a different way."

"How's it different?"

"Well, it's. . . ."

"Deeper?"

"Just different."

"Who do you love more, Jesus or Elvis?"

"That's a stupid question."

But that's the thing. It isn't all that stupid a question. A few days ago we were at an Elvis seminar at Memphis University, an auditorium of people gathered for a panel to talk about the impact Elvis had on their lives. All the old Memphis mob was there. The room smelled of hairnet and Kung Fu aftershave. Person after person got up and talked about Elvis. The audience shouted hallelujahs and applauded wildly at absolutely anything the speakers said.

Then, Elvis's former nurse, Mrs. Cox, stood up at the podium to speak: "Although Elvis was great, God love him, he was still human, and by human, I mean that he was not God. He was not the son of God, either. Elvis didn't like being called the King," she said. "Jesus was the real King. Elvis always knew he was less important than Jesus."

There was an awkward silence in the hall. People didn't know how to respond. Sure, they knew it was true, but did she have to go and say it like that? It seemed so cold. Maybe sacreligious.

Elvis, to my mind, was not a class act. So he gave away a few candies. He was the kind of guy who would have leapt at the chance to appear on THE MUPPET SHOW, calling Miss Piggy "mama" and sending Scooter out for Thorazine and Percodan.

Where does Elvis situate himself in the vast pantheon of Jewish entertainers? Don Rickles, the playful uncle who insists on goosing his nephews after every punchline; Jerry Lewis, the sullen carpet salesman who silently eats his gefilte fish at the seder table, drunkenly piping up occasionally with vitriolic lines like, "Never mind what the U.S. did for the Jews! What did the Jews do for the Jews?"; Phyllis Diller, the well-meaning auntie, shushing him down with another plate of verenikas; the great Marty Feldman; the bizarre bachelor and proofreader at the Jewish Suburban who pours over the Haggadah all night looking for typos. Where does Elvis find himself in this? Sitting at the children's table beside the nebbish Barry Manilow fighting over the last misshapen Jewish meatball that has rolled free onto the "special" plastic table cloth? Reclining in his folding chair, his massive gold Champion of the World belt unbuckled, chewing on a toothpick, nodding his head empathetically to Shecky Greene's umpteenth story that always ends with his "shnagging" a cocktail waitress in the hat check. What does poor Elvis need from that? He has his own problems.

It might seem silly to us that these people worship Elvis. But 2000 years from now, who knows? Anyway, he's just as valid a choice of icon as anybody else. He makes them feel good, he does good deeds. And he's a god that can sing and dance. That's nice, right? That's got to be a bonus.

GRACELAND, PARKING LOT.

Jonathan interviews a woman.

JONATHAN: What kind of a role does Elvis play in your life?
WOMAN: I have an Elvis room in my house. That's where I keep all my Elvis stuff. And last October my niece died and she had an Elvis funeral.
JONATHAN: God. What does that mean, an Elvis funeral?
WOMAN: We did it just the way Elvis had his. We played Elvis songs and we tied yellow ribbons around everything. In the casket, we had her dressed up just like Elvis. She was dying of cancer and it was the way she wanted it to be.

BEALE STREET, MEMPHIS.

The legendary Memphis street, where Elvis, B.B. King and Jerry Lee Lewis went to see black blues musicians perform, is now a tourist mecca.

EVAN (*to Schmelvis*): Make sure the people react to you. Get in their faces.
SCHMELVIS: Yeah, I know what you want. You want somebody to jump me like a dog and kick the crap out of me. Then you'd be happy. That'd make for some good footage.
EVAN: Schmel, how can you say that? I would never wish that upon you.
SCHMELVIS: Yeah, well you can take the suit and shove it up your ass.

(Schmelvis walks away.)

EVAN (*turning to Jonathan*): Well, Jon. It looks like it's going to be up to you tonight to get some reaction. Schmelvis doesn't seem to be in the right mood.
JONATHAN: It's simple, really. We just got to go find ourselves some rednecks. We're in the Deep South. How hard can that be? Who looks like they'll just punch my face in?

(He walks up to a man.)

JONATHAN: Excuse me, we've uncovered some evidence that Elvis
Presley was Jewish. What do you think?
MAN: I don't know if he was Jewish or not.
JONATHAN: Let's say for the sake of argument that he was Jewish.
Shouldn't that mean anything?
MAN: Why, have you got something against Jews?
JONATHAN: No.
MAN: Well, I haven't either.

ZUCCHINI ELVIS!

SEATTLE, WA—Seattle gardener Delroy Sykes was shocked to discover a zuchini growing in his garden that bore a striking and eerie resemblance to the late, great King himself.

"I was choked up and misty-eyed," Sykes said. "It was like a message from Elvis himself saying to me everything would be okay in the world. I ran inside and showed it to my wife, Laurie Ray. She said it looked more like Wayne Newton. I told her, no way. Wayne Newton may have played Vegas, but he was no King. And and there was no mistaking those sideburns and sunglasses. This was truly a zucchini grown in the image and likeness of Elvis."

When asked what became of the Zuchini-Elvis, he replied, "Well, I wanted to put it on display somewhere . . . you know like them holy places . . . sort of a shrine. But the wife said no. Said people would think I was addlebrained. I may hear the occasional voice or two, but I don't want anyone thinking that all my dogs ain't barkin' up the same tree, if you follow me. So I gave Zuchini-Elvis to the wife and she made it into zucchini bread. I ate it with peanut butter and bananas like the King would have wanted me to. Tasted okay. Kinda sad to see it go. But I took a picture of it."

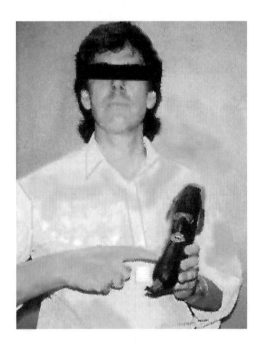

REPORTER: What's your role as the writer and director of this film?

MAX: All I've got to do is get these guys out there screwing around and this stuff writes itself.

REPORTER: Sort of like a Monkees movie?

MAX: Yeah, I guess. I've never seen one of those, but I'm assuming that people liked the Monkees, right?

REPORTER: Sure.

MAX: Well, okay, like the Monkees, except without the part about people liking them. Nobody's going to like these guys because they're nasty and selfish. They're vastly unlikable.

REPORTER: So maybe more like the Sex Pistols than the Monkees.

MAX: But the Sex Pistols had some kind of appeal, right. They were filling some kind of niche or other. They had something that you could describe as a talent, right?

REPORTER: Sure, they were really talented.

MAX: Well, these guys have none of that. They have nothing.

REPORTER: Wow, that's pretty nihilistic.

MAX: And they work cheap, too.

Director's Log, Aug. 18, 2000

When we set out for Memphis, we thought we would find a city seething with rednecks pissed off to discover Elvis was a Jew. That was supposed to provide the film with its real drama.

But when we got here, something odd happened. Every southerner and Elvis fan we met, except Jerry Falwell's goddaughter, was kind, tolerant, and completely the opposite of every stereotype we had ever encountered.

Before we got here, we believed all the stories we had read about Elvis—that he was a fat, bloated, white trash caricature who had stolen all his music from black musicians.

Within days, however, we discovered that's all a load of crap. By all accounts, Elvis was a truly good guy—the victim of the evil Colonel Tom and the parasitical hangers-on who ruined his life and wasted his talent. He grew up poor in the Jim Crow South and by all rights he should have been a redneck. Instead, he resisted all the nastiness around him and clung to the values his mother had instilled in him. He didn't have a racist bone in his body and, contrary to popular belief, he gave full credit to the black musicians who influenced his music.

Today it dawned on me . . . we are the actual rednecks. It's a little disconcerting.

Postcard from Graceland Memorial Gardens
Memphis, Mississippi

Debbie, I started off thinking it was a mitzvah, this trip, now I'm not so sure. I thought that I could elevate this whole thing, offer a little something more. Now I know that I have failed. It's like they've made me into an animal just like they are. Are they stronger than me? I have to look to God. I have to ask for strength from the almighty. That's the only strength, the strength that God gives you. The Winnebago smells so bad. It's become the gateway to Gehenna. It smells like the devil. It smells of lies. I can open all the windows, and still this horrible smell. There is an onion being unravelled. Every day a new skin is removed, and we are left with something smaller and still just as mysterious. And dear lord! What a stink this onion has.

xoxo

Dan

Who does Rabbi Poupko remind you of?

JONATHAN: He has the gruffness of Abe Vigoda coupled with the hairy-backed vulnerability of a young Anthony Quinn.

ARI: He reminds me of my uncle Hymie. Hymie was a nice guy, but when he drank he got sort of surly. I guess he reminds me of my old uncle Hymie when he was really drunk. Which isn't to say that Rabbi Poupko is a drinker. To the best of my knowledge he isn't.

SCHMELVIS: Richard Dreyfuss with none of the redeeming warmth.

EVAN: Krusty the Clown and a meat blender.

DAN: He reminds me of a lot of people. A lot of people I ended up punching in the face. He also reminds me of this guy I dangled off a balcony during spring break. True story.

MAX: Rabbi Poupko is a little like Sgt. Rock from the comic books, leading us into battle. He's also got a little Ron Jeremy to him. And a hell of a lot of Don Rickles.

MILA: Rabbi Poupko is a very sad character. He reminds me of Woody Allen when he gets all sad and quiet.

Evan fights with every person on the crew.

MILA: Mila's like a silent Miss Little Bo Peep with everyone and then with me he's Mr. Alpha Male. He doesn't realize that I'm the only one on his side. If it was up to Max, the whole thing would be shot on Polaroids and we'd have a slide show at Sundance. There's Mila always staring, always judging. I'd like to cram that camera up his ass. It's not like I don't want to help him carry the equipment, but it's 100 percent his responsibility. That was a part of the agreement. Now, if I offer, that's one thing. But when he turns and looks at me like he's Christ on the cross as he's waddling down the street with bags hanging off his back, like I'm the Roman asshole soldier trying to kill him, that's what makes me sick. I have no patience for that.

ARI: Mr. Nice Guy. Mr. Nice Guys should be working with lepers, not on films.

DAN: Dan's always trying to stick us for more money. The first night in Memphis, him and Mila end up blowing all of their per diems across the street from the motel at some dive, buying drinks for every rummy and barfly in the city. Dan isn't happy unless everyone's fighting. When that happens, he sits off to the side, wise and stoic, fiddling with his battery pack, like a true goddam professional with the world on a string.

MAX: Max is like the Gestapo, kicking our fucking door in at 6 a.m. every morning, like if he wasn't there nothing would get done. There he is eating a thirty pound watermelon with a fork and knife by himself at a picnic table, meticulously cutting the thing into one-inch squares like the Dean of Eton eating British meatloaf on All Saints' Day.

JONATHAN: I just say what he's thinking, and he knows it, and then I'm the asshole.

Evan and Jonathan discuss Schmelvis's growing megolamania in the Winnebago as Johnny Cash music plays.

AT THE BACK OF THE WINNEBAGO

JONATHAN: He really thinks this is going to make him a star?

EVAN: Max told him that some Elvis impersonators can make $300,000 a year and get treated like Elvis himself, limos, the whole shebang. He thinks he's going to be one of those.

JONATHAN: How can that be?

EVAN: Look, he's taken time away from a very successful career as a day trader to run around in a polyester jump suit; of course he thinks he's going to make a fortune.

JONATHAN: God, that's terrible.

EVAN: He's the worst Elvis impersonator I've ever seen.

JONATHAN: Maybe we can get someone to put on a fake beard and replace him, sort of like what Ed Wood did when Bela Lugosi died during the filming of *Plan Nine From Outer Space.* We can have him keep his Elvis cape in front of his face as he walks down the street.

Schmelvis needed a place to stay on the Sabbath so he hooked up with this Memphis rabbi, who invited him to spend the weekend. It turns out this Rabbi knew a little girl who was recovering from cancer. She was from Venezuela and she had flown in for treatment at the Danny Thomas Children's Hospital in Memphis. The kid was religious and she was just crazy about Elvis. The Make-a-Wish Foundation came over and asked her what was her greatest wish. She said, "My father says to ask for our whole family to fly to Israel." The woman responded, "Yes, but what is your wish?"

The girl thought for a moment and said, "To meet Elvis." She didn't know he was dead.

So the family arranges for Schmelvis to go over there to play for the girl and her friends. He said that he would go there himself and that we should pick him up at 8 p.m.

The night we pulled into the Rabbi's driveway to pick Schmelvis up, Evan was driving and we almost destroyed the family's station wagon. We could hear from the front porch that Schmelvis was still playing in there. We watched through the lit picture window as he entertained them, singing "Hava Nagila" and whatnot. They were eating it up. It was like he could do no wrong.

Dan said that he was finally among his people.

When Schmelvis finally came out he was in a sweat.

"Look at my fingers," he said.

They were bleeding.

"It's a nice thing you did," said Dan.

Ari writes a poem in the Winnebago bathroom:

we whizz along
this family
of screwy uncles
with hunchbacks
and cameras
searching for America.
Can you believe it?
that is what we are doing
us guys
we are looking for America

What Ari's snoring reminds people of:

EVAN: A drugged ferret protecting its young from predators
SCHMELVIS: A Zamboni that's fallen over
JONATHAN: A circus strong man being choked to death
MAX: An otter caught in a bear trap gnawing its own leg off
MILA: An underwater electric chain saw
DAN: Experimental jazz

Ari on the importance of good vibes

I don't care what anyone tells you. The most important thing in life is good vibes. It's good vibes that keeps life afloat. The second you lose that, you're going down the tubes. I try to keep the good vibes going but I feel like I'm in this thing alone and I'm fed up.

All day Ari is such a nice guy, and he really is a nice guy. Really. Like, if you had a twisted ankle or something, Ari would piggyback you around all day long. Even if you pretended you had a twisted ankle, and he was 90 percent certain you were full of shit, he would give you the benefit of the doubt and haul you around on his back. And even if afterwards you told him, straight out, that you'd been lying, that there was no hurt ankle, he would probably chalk it up to some emotional turmoil you were going through and he would still feel sorry for you, and still lug your fat-assed unhurt ankle all over Memphis. Don't ask me how I know this. I just do.

But where does all his rage go? I know there is rage. How could there not be? At night, in the motel, Evan and I recorded his snoring and pretended we were British explorers on some safari hunt stalking some growly feline in its lair. We played it for everyone. Even Ari. He just smiled. But there was a lot of rage in that snoring. You could hear it.

At night, while we're all asleep, I imagine him out in the hotel parking lot, over at the far end, near the dumpsters, holding onto some poor homeless bum's lapel, and stabbing him, over and over and over, right through the chest and stomach, all through the night, and by sunrise, coming back into the hotel room, fresh, ready to begin the day, the nicest guy in the world.

Director's Log, Aug. 16, 2000 — Research Notes

As if the Presleytarian Church of Elvis the Divine wasn't enough, today we ran into the leader of another Elvis Church, which appears to have a competing theology. I wonder if he went up to Graceland like Martin Luther and tacked the doctrine to the gates.

THE FIRST CHURCH OF CHRIST, ELVIS

"For unto you is born this day in the city of Memphis a Presley, which is Elvis the King."

And Elvis saw them berating the poor recording artist, whose music was terrible and lyrics insipid, and Lo, the King said unto the mob: "Let him who is without bad singles cast the first rhinestone." And the mob turned down their eyes, each considering his own "Don't Worry Be Happy" or "Man in the Mirror" and shuffled off.

"Thank you," said Elvis. "Thank you very much."

And I turned to see the voice that spake with me. And being turned, I saw seven golden records; and in the midst of the seven golden records one like unto the Son of Zeke, clothed with a jumpsuit down to the foot, and girthed . . . er . . . girt about the paunch with rhinestones. His hairs were black like vinyl, as black as Brylcream; and his eyes, how they twinkled, his dimples, how merry. Who is this King of Rock'n'Roll? The Lord of Hostess, he is the King of Rock'n'Roll. Shaboom.

And Elvis so loved the world that he died, fat and bloated, in a bathroom. He very pointedly did not rise from the dead three days later, but was nonetheless seen across the world by various and sundry housewives. Create your own "Ain't Nuthin' Butta Hound-Dogmas," but be sure to like stars in the night, make each a "Hunka Hunka Burnin' Love."

"Return, we beseech thee, O Lord of Hostess: look down from Heaven, and behold, and visit this mall."

Part 3

Back in Montreal

From: Ari Cohen <aricohen@diversus.com>
To: emb@diversus.com
Sent: Mon 10/7/00 2:19 AM
Subject: screwed
Attachment:

been going through the footage day and night with the editor and all I can think every second that i'm watching is: where's the film? where's the beginning, because films have beginnings? where's the end? ends are satisfying. "yes. elvis was a jew. THE END." that's an ending. what we have is a pile of shit. at least heaven's gate had kris kristofferson. what do we have? we have nothing. i should have had my head examined for listening to you. and by the way, the car rental charged us an additional $1400 in damages. who the fuck stole all the cutlery? did you know we were supposed to empty the toilet tank every so often? i'm never setting foot on a winnebago as long as I live.

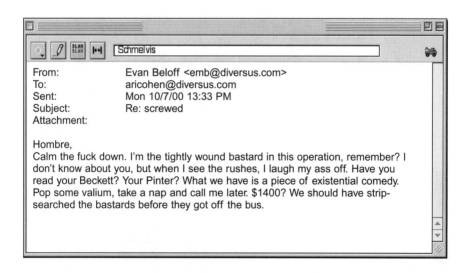

Schmelvis

From: Evan Beloff <emb@diversus.com>
To: aricohen@diversus.com
Sent: Mon 10/7/00 13:33 PM
Subject: Re: screwed
Attachment:

Hombre,
Calm the fuck down. I'm the tightly wound bastard in this operation, remember? I don't know about you, but when I see the rushes, I laugh my ass off. Have you read your Beckett? Your Pinter? What we have is a piece of existential comedy. Pop some valium, take a nap and call me later. $1400? We should have strip-searched the bastards before they got off the bus.

From: Evan Beloff <emb@diversus.com>
To: maxwallace@email.com
Sent: Mon 10/7/00 13:45 PM
Subject:
Attachment:

Max, Ari's freaking out. Maybe's he's right. We don't really have a film here. It's just a bunch of scenes of me navel-gazing about my Jewish identity.

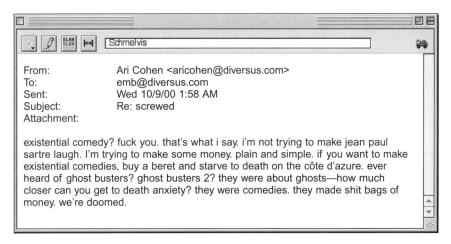

From: Ari Cohen <aricohen@diversus.com>
To: emb@diversus.com
Sent: Wed 10/9/00 1:58 AM
Subject: Re: screwed
Attachment:

existential comedy? fuck you. that's what i say. i'm not trying to make jean paul sartre laugh. I'm trying to make some money. plain and simple. if you want to make existential comedies, buy a beret and starve to death on the côte d'azure. ever heard of ghost busters? ghost busters 2? they were about ghosts—how much closer can you get to death anxiety? they were comedies. they made shit bags of money. we're doomed.

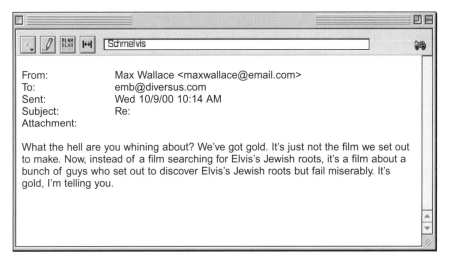

From: Max Wallace <maxwallace@email.com>
To: emb@diversus.com
Sent: Wed 10/9/00 10:14 AM
Subject: Re:
Attachment:

What the hell are you whining about? We've got gold. It's just not the film we set out to make. Now, instead of a film searching for Elvis's Jewish roots, it's a film about a bunch of guys who set out to discover Elvis's Jewish roots but fail miserably. It's gold, I'm telling you.

Ari's drunk poem (written in the Diversus office at 3 a.m.)

why do we make movies?

we are ghosts
me and you
you see that?
we have a problem
how we want to be
and how we want to be
and we spend some money
but what is money?
when you're a ghost
let me explain:
once there were ghosts
and they yelled and yelled
but that's still what they were
not even that loud
and then they tightened their stomachs
and got so hard
but still

From: Max Wallace <maxwallace@email.com
To: aricohen@diversus.com, emb@diversus.com
Sent: Fri 10/11/00 11:19 PM
Subject: Israel
Attachment:

Okay. There's not enough material from the Memphis trip to justify a feature-length documentary. But you know how as Jews we're always being told that our roots are in Israel? Well, what better place to look for Elvis's roots than in the Holy Land? Picture it: camels, desert, Arabs, falafel. For all we know, Elvis is really working on a Kibbutz over there and we'll get the exclusive footage. That'll put some goddam shekels in your pocket, no? Seriously, there's a place outside Jerusalem called the Elvis Inn — a virtual shrine to the King — with the world's biggest Elvis statue. We won't even have to worry anymore about finding kosher restaurants for Schmelvis. What do you say? If we don't do this, we don't have a film and Pearlie will tear Evan a new asshole with her kosher carving knife.

On the plane to Israel, during turbulence, Jonathan thinks:

What will their faces look like as we nosedive to the ground? Will Ari clutch my knee? Will Evan stand before me in the aisle, naked, stripped of all irony? Will we claw at each other for Schmelvis's tfillin bag, for one last chance at redemption before we vanish for all time?

DAY 1

ISRAEL, TEL AVIV AIRPORT.

The crew exits the airplane. Schmelvis drops to his knees and kisses the ground.

EVAN: What are you doing?
SCHMELVIS: What's it look like? I'm kissing the earth.
EVAN: First of all, you're kissing a concrete runway that one of those flag guys probably has peed on. Secondly, you look like you're bowing to Mila.
MAX: Get out of the frame, Evan. It's a nice shot. Kissing the ground will be good for the opening Israeli montage.
EVAN: How about we get a shot of you kissing my ass? Will that work for the montage?
JONATHAN: We've been in the Holy Land not more than seven minutes and already you're hostile.

Jonathan's notes towards a novel he will never finish

I'm standing in front of the Wailing Wall. There are notes scrawled on little bits of paper, ripped cigarette packs, Kleenex — you name it — all crammed into the cracks of the wall. Crammed in there tight, like mortar. I just want to pick them all free and read them. What a great book that would make. Or, what a pile of crap, 300 pages of "I want to get laid. I want more money." A famous Israeli poet once said that the air in Jerusalem is thick with yearning. The mortar in the wall has been replaced by mute cries.

I've written down a blessing and I've filled the paper with every single person I've ever met. I'm blessing everybody, even people that I can hardly stand. Everybody deserves a blessing. Even the ones who don't deserve it. It makes me feel good to bless them. It makes me feel high and mighty, like I'm standing on top of the wall itself, looking down on every one, spitting and dropping pennies. I finish writing and look for a piece of crack to cram. There are none. I need to get higher. I call over Evan.

"What?"

I start scaling his back to gain some leverage. In the process, his hat and sunglasses fall off.

"What are you doing?" he yells.

"I'm trying to bless you. I'm actually trying to bless all of us."

He throws me against the wall, the wall heavy with all of our hope, our begging, our blessing.

At the Wailing Wall

EVAN: I turn around and Schmelvis is clinging to my back like dirty sheet pimples. I feel like I'm in a leather bondage video. He's wrapping and I'm running. "It's not just the blacks who rap," he's yelling in my ear, his beard reeking of tuna and boiled eggs. No thanks. I swear I'm going to be a Buddhist after this trip. He's like a cross between the *alteh rebbe* and an insurance salesman. But it's not money and policies he wants. It's mitzvahs. I've never met anyone as greedy for mitzvahs in my life. The only worse experience I ever had at the Wall was the time I accidentally started praying on the women's side and a big fat Russian woman in a babushka smacked me in the back of the head.

ARI: I guess it's nice, right? It seems to make him really happy and it's not much of a sweat for me. I put on *tfillin* once and a while, anyway. I gotta say, though, he does wrap it a little too tight. After a while, I thought my hand was starting to fall asleep, and then it felt like I had gangrene. He said the tighter the better, but fuck, I felt like blood was going to start pouring out from under my finger nails.

DAN: He could have at least allowed me the experience. Wrap me up in it just so I don't have to feel like hire-a-goy.

MAX: There's no way I'm putting that thing on. Plain and simple. He'd have to stab me in the ass with a tranquilizer dart and lay me out on the ground.

JONATHAN: Wrapping yourself in *tfillin* is really one of the most blatantly absurd of God's laws. And that's what makes it so beautiful, in a way. Unlike, say, giving *tzadakeh* (Jewish charity) which has obvious, immediately observable social merits, putting on *tfillin* is so out there. It's so removed from what we can see as positive in any conceivable context. Men do it because God told them to. And that's it. No other reason. That's why you're supposed to do any mitzvah, really. But the other ones have pleasant ramifications on some level. Like not eating meat with milk meant you weren't as likely to contact some kind of food disease; but doing something simply because you believe your God has instructed you to do so is as deep as it gets. On the other hand, putting on *tfillin* because a *Chassidic* Elvis impersonator has told you to do so makes you feel like a sack of crap. I'm just saying.

MILA: I'm just glad I'm carrying the camera. Thank God they just leave me alone. It's like they just see right through me. When they look into the camera, they get that thousand-mile stare, like they're looking right into the eyes of their adoring fans.

JERUSALEM, HAISHA TORAH.

Rabbi Poupko insisted on taking the group on a tour of Evan's old yeshiva. The rabbi begins asking every yeshiva boy going in or out the same question.

RABBI: Did you know Elvis was Jewish?
YESHIVA STUDENT #1: The Jews like to claim everybody so I'm always skeptical about these things.
RABBI: Do you know any Elvis songs?
STUDENT: Something about a hound dog, right?
RABBI: And in singing "You Ain't Nothin' but a Hound Dog,"don't you think he was singing about the plight of the Diaspora Jew? It's possible, right?
YESHIVA STUDENT #1: Okay.
RABBI: Give us a little Elvis. Give us a little "Hound Dog."

(He starts clapping his hands.)

YESHIVA STUDENT #1: No thanks.
RABBI: You boys are out of touch with the world of the body. It's not all about living in the brain.
YESHIVA STUDENT #1 (*not dancing*): So what's so important about Elvis being a Jew anyway?
RABBI: Elvis is the prism through which we analyze Jewish identity.
YESHIVA STUDENT #1: Good luck.

(The student leaves and the rabbi grabs another STUDENT.)

RABBI: Did you know Elvis was Jewish?
YESHIVA STUDENT #2: DeNiro is.
RABBI: Who?
YESHIVA STUDENT #1: Robert DeNiro
RABBI: I just heard that. His mother was Jewish, his father was Italian. How did you know that?
YESHIVA STUDENT #1: I'm related to him.
RABBI: He's related to DeNiro. Can you do the DeNiro thing? (*putting on an accent*) Are you talking to me?

DIRECTOR'S LOG

The Rabbi has this encyclopedic knowledge of every obscure famous Jew in show-business. I think that's why this film appealed to him. He kept rattling off all these unlikely names that were supposed to be Jewish: Marilyn Monroe, Audrey Hepburn, Cary Grant, DeNiro. When he met the guy who claimed to be related to DeNiro, he acted like he had just met Moses himself. (FOR COMPLETE LIST OF FAMOUS JEWS, SEE APPENDIX).

23 JERUSALEM, HAISHA TORAH. CONTINUOUS.

Evan interviews a yeshiva STUDENT.

EVAN: So when was the last time you got some action?
JONATHAN: What the hell's the matter with you? Are you nuts?
Please excuse my friend. It looks like his haircut has gone
to his head.
YESHIVA STUDENT #3: It's alright. I have all the action I need
right here.
EVAN: A little of the old ass-jockey-ball-hockey. I got you.
That's why I got out while I could. I'd be *essing schnitzel* too
if I stuck around.
JONATHAN: Wow, what an animal.
YESHIVA STUDENT #3: You used to go here, huh?
EVAN: Yeah, I used to go here. I was here for six months. I know
the drill.

Why I went to Yeshiva

by Evan M. Beloff

I went on an all-expenses-paid fellowship program to Israel. A "cultural and political trip," they called it. There was no mention of yeshiva — it was clearly a Zionist indoctrination trip — but after a few months of travel, many of the fellowship recipients decided to stay and learn and become religious.

"Stay, brother," they said, but I had to return home. I was about to begin my first semester of university and my father had died just eight months earlier. I needed to be home.

But then I didn't want to be home. I didn't want any of it. Yeshiva seemed like my only option.

They put me in a room that overlooked the Wailing Wall. My first night in the Jewish Quarter, I jumped out of bed at 3 a.m. scared awake by the sounds of Arab prayers. I didn't know it was a regular ritual. I thought it was a call to holy war.

The daily drill was up for prayer at 7 a.m.; learn all day in the study rooms until late into the evening with one hour for breakfast and 45 minutes for lunch; and after dinner, there was some form of lecture or programming.

Of course, I had my own ritual which was to miss prayers, go to class at 10 a.m., skip lunch and come back to siesta in my dorm until 2 p.m., then return to class; skip dinner, go out on the town and party and drink tequila and try to sleep with Israeli women; return by cab at 4 a.m. and start the torah process all over again around 9:55 a.m.

I thrived on reconciling the contradictions. Embrace opposites was my motto. I can still remember my rabbi pointing his finger in my face, promising me a pretty vegetarian wife if I just stayed and when I wouldn't, he blurted out: "You know your problem? You'll never be religious because you're too damn emotional. Religion isn't emotional!"

We stumbled upon a shop that has the Bible Code software that claims to unravel the hidden codes embedded in the Old Testament which prophesied many famous historical events and figures. So, we go in and ask them if they can find Elvis in the Bible. The guy punches in Elvis in Hebrew and his name comes up sixty-one times, intersecting with the word "Jew" twenty times. Everybody is impressed.

"Isn't that something?" Evan says to me after the Bible Code demonstration, with his Prince Valiant haircut and Sheriff of Nottingham goatee. "That is undeniably something. Even a heathen like you has to see it. You'd have to be blind not to see it."

Evan is genuinely impressed. Seeing him impressed is a frightening sight. I like him better filled with impotent rage.

We have turned up so little evidence, we are turning to the bible. What next? Tarot cards? Tea leaf reading? "The bottom of my cup looks like Elvis spinning a dreydle." We're doomed.

Leaving Bible Code Store

EVAN (to Jonathan): What do you think of that? We've finally got something. Elvis's name appearing 61 times in the Bible!

JONATHAN: Yeah, but I think Ernest Borgnine's name appears in there eighty-one odd times as well, so really what does it prove?

Evan calls his Aunt Pearlie because he said he would

Auntie Pearlie. It's Evan. Yeah. Because I told you I would. Because I said I was going to call you. You think I'm not a man of my word? Then why are you acting so surprised? Sure it's going well. Yes, I'm very glad we came here. Not a single regret. Well, we've been gathering a lot of evidence. That's right. We're reading the bible for clues. It's a very long and involved process. I'll explain in Montreal. I put a blessing in the wall for you. I asked Hashem to cure your arthritis. It's worth a shot, no? Doesn't cost you anything, right? I better go Auntie Pearlie.

DAY 2

24 JERUSALEM, PROMENADE OVERLOOKING THE CITY.

Evan, Jonathan and Dan make small talk while enjoying the view.

JONATHAN: Rabbi Poupko is like the priest in *On the Waterfront*. Hangs out in bars, chain smokes, and still leads sermon on Sundays.

EVAN: Say what you want about him, he may be cynical but he doesn't try to force people to believe. Schmelvis, on the other hand, is a guy who's just returned to religion. He thinks he'll score brownie points by converting us.

DAN: You know, I just got to say, that out of all of you, Schmelvis is the only one who actually cares about me and Mila. He asks how we're feeling, he gives you a cigarette, water. He's the only one that bothered to explain anything to me. This is the center of his universe. (*pointing to the city*) He's just happy to be here and he's trying to share it with you guys.

EVAN: I don't have anything against him. I just resent the missionizing. It's driving the rabbi crazy.

DAN: Yeah, that isn't going so hot, between the Rabbi and Schmelvis. Each one thinks the other's a dummy.

EVAN: There's a little tension.

JONATHAN: A little tension? Let me recap. First, Schmelvis told him to start acting like a Rabbi intead of a rodeo clown. Then the Rabbi told him that he has b.o. Then Schmelvis tells him he wants to break a bottle over his head.

EVAN: You need that kind of back and forth in a documentary. You need a little conflict. You can't have everyone standing around patting each other on the back. Where's the fun in that?

JONATHAN: Right. In *Gimme Shelter* you had the Hell's Angels. We have a defrocked rabbi.

EVAN: He's not a defrocked Rabbi. I don't even think you can defrock a rabbi.

JONATHAN: The Jews have their own way of doing things. Look at Spinoza. One day he showed up to synagogue and the congregation was dancing a *hora* on his spine at the entrance of the shul. Before this whole movie Schmelvis had a lot of reverence and respect for the rabbi. Now they can hardly be in the same room. Do you think there's still a little love between them?

EVAN: Absolutely not. There's no love at all.

DAN: Just think of how good he was with those old people at the nursing home the next time you feel like bashing Schmelvis.

JONATHAN: Yeah, he really connects with old people. I think he's really sincere about that. Here's an interesting parallel. When Elvis would perform, women would literally pass out. Just think about having that kind of power over women where you can actually make them pass out. And when Schmelvis performs at the old age home, there's people passing out left and right....

Director's Log, Nov. 1, 2000

We went to The Elvis Inn, a gas station/café outside Jerusalem which is basically a shrine to Elvis. Outside is the world's largest Elvis statue. We meet the owner, Uri Yoeli, an Israeli who explains he saw Elvis perform in Salt Lake City in 1972 and saw Elvis with a *chai* around his neck and it inspired him to open the Elvis Inn. It receives 2 million visitors a year, making it Israel's second-largest tourist attraction, after the Wailing Wall.

"Do you serve kosher peanut butter and banana sandwiches here?" Schmelvis asked him.

"The Israelis, they don't like that."

"Can you serve one for Schmelvis?"

"Absolutely."

Outside, a bus full of Palestinian children arrive on a day trip from the Gaza Strip. When they see Schmelvis, they go crazy. Their teacher asks Schmelvis to sing for the children. He climbs up on the statue and sings. The Arab children go nuts, swarming around him, playing drums and singing with him. Their teacher stands beside me and surveys the scene of an Orthodox Jewish Elvis impersonator bonding with Arab schoolchildren.

"Elvis brings peace through the children," said the teacher.

"Will you say that on camera?" I asked her.

"I can't. I would be in grave danger."

Schmelvis boards the bus to say goodbye to the children. "You've been a wonderful audience. Thank you very much."

Schmelvis has become his own polyester Middle East peace plan.

ARI: I should have asked out that girl in the T-shirt shop. She was cute. I could have definitely talked a little more with her. Shit, man. I could go back, but ah, that would seem weird. I could tell her that I just realized I once had a dream about her. I only realized it once I was walking away. But then I'd have to hurry back really fast. I'd have to go back right this second. I'd have to show up back there doing a kind of half trot. I'd have to start talking to her while I was still trotting, trotting with a big smile on my face, this big "I just have to tell you" smile on my face. I can't do that. If I go back tomorrow, I could bring her a poem telling her that her smile brings wind to the streets of Jerusalem. What a sleazy thing to say. I think she might have liked me, too.

MILA: Saturday night. A group of sixteen-year-old girls go by. They're dressed up for a night on the town. They've got M16's slung over their backs because everybody in Israel has to do militray service. They go into a bar and I follow them. I've got my camera and I want some pictures. I ask them if I can get some shots. They're all into it. They pose with the guns. They strike all these Charlie's Angels poses. They're really cute. It's so terrible. They're all trying to be cute. I'm smiling and snapping off as many pictures as I can. It's like *Beverly Hills 90210* with guns.

DAN: I'm wrapped in wires in the fucking desert heat. If I was a techy for a British techno band my name would be Wires. The lead singer, stringy, floppy, alternative hair flopped over one eye, would holler at me, "Hey, Wires, get this shit set up. Sound check, m'man." It isn't a good look for me, the wires and the sweat. It makes me look like a hyperventilating bulldog. A bulldog tangled in wire. I could have been a contender, instead I'm a big, sweaty, tech-boy in shorts and boxers riding up his ass in a cardboard yarmulke taking orders from insurance shysters with artistic aspirations. The rational is always, "it's funny." Hey, I just took a crap on your shoes. Isn't that funny? There's some humor for you.

Jonathan's Journal

The rabbi tells everyone in the car about why Israel has to stand up to the Palestinian terrorists. How there's no choice really. He talks for a good half hour as the car drives along. He knows a lot. Everyone listens. There's no one in the car who knows more than he does. He speaks with a lot of passion. Evan says that Poupko often starts crying because of all of his passion. He tells us the history of Israel. There's no doubt about it. Rabbi Poupko is a Zionist.

"If you walk through the Arab quarters like a mealy-mouthed Diaspora Jew with your tail between your legs, then they're going to want to slit your throat. Christ, I'd wanna slit your throat. But if you walk in there like a proud Jew, then you'll be fine."

When we get out of the car, I ask Rabbi Poupko if there was a war whether he would want his son to go off and fight.

He pauses for a second. "I would," he says.

Schmelvis is hardly the first ethnic Elvis tribute artist to pay homage to the King. He isn't even the first to coin the name Schmelvis. That distinction belongs to Don Martin of *Mad Magazine* who created the character "Shmelvis Parsley" in the mid-70s.

MELVIS

 Laying claim to being the very first Jewish Elvis impersonator, Melvis calls himself the Kosher King of Rock'n'Roll. Among the more elderly Elvis tribute artists working, Melvis focuses his act on the later (fat and medicated) Elvis. No longer a teenager, Melvis has had to cut back his number of live performances due to the demands and rigors of life on the road. Melvis just isn't as regular as he once was and his condition is not improving. Nowadays he's looking for endorsements from Depends, Centrum, Tums, and the like. Melvis hopes to hit the road again for a special anniversary tour to perform his standards:

(I'm just a) Gigolo

That Was Your Daughter?

Shake Your Waist 'til it Dislocates

Blue Suede Jews

Ain't No Gums Like Your Gums Baby

Love Me Like a Gentile

Whose Bed Pan is That?

Never Whine Before it's Time

Pass the Pepto

EL VEZ

 Probably the most famous of all Elvis tribute artists is Robert Lopez, a.k.a. El Vez, the Mexican Elvis impersonator. Born in Chula Vista, California, El Vez grew up an Elvis Presley fan who believed the King was, in fact, Latino.

In 60s films like *Roustabout* and *Fun in Acapulco*, he explains, "Elvis wore continental slacks and had slicked-back hair and dark good looks. He looked like my uncles. So I thought, oh, Elvis must be Latino, too."

A veteran of the Southern California punk-era bands the Zeroes and Catholic

Discipline, El Vez says the idea for his alter ego sprang from a month-long exhibit of Elvis-inspired art he curated at a Mexican folk art gallery in Los Angeles in 1988. Before long, he was guesting on the *Tonight Show*, singing such standards as "You Ain't Nothing But a Cucaracha" with his band, the Memphis Mariachis.

Among his repertoire of albums—which combine Latino parodies of Elvis songs with political satire—is the bestseller *Graciasland*, which includes singles, "Esta Buena Mamacita (That's All Right Mama)"and "Say it Loud! I'm Brown and I'm Proud."

TORTELVIS

 And of course there's Tortelvis, the 300-pound lead singer for the band Dread Zeppelin, which has been described as a cross between Elvis Presley, Bob Marley, and Led Zeppelin. Tortelvis, whose real name is Greg Tortell, kicked off his career on January 8, 1989 on what would have been the King's 54th birthday.

JERUSALEM, BEN YEHUDA PEDESTRIAN MALL.

The crew munches on burgers and fries from Burger King. Evan tries to convince Schmelvis to perform.

SCHMELVIS: It would be bad for the Schmelvis image, busking.
EVAN: We're not busking. We're not playing for money. Well, we are playing for money, but we're not busking.
SCHMELVIS (*annoyed*): How's playing on the street for money not busking? You want me to busk.
EVAN: When Elvis played sold out shows for money, was that busking?
SCHMELVIS: That was indoors. I'm standing out here with my hand out like a *schnorer*.
EVAN: Where's your *chouach*? I'm not asking you to dance for shekels. This is really quite lovely. Look. We're already drawing a crowd.
SCHMELVIS: Of course we're drawing a crowd. A man in a skin-tight polyester jump suit in the middle of a screaming match will always draw a crowd. That's entertainment!
EVAN (*to Rabbi Poupko*): Will you talk to him?
RABBI (*in between bites of his kosher Whopper*): Elvis had Vegas. Schmelvis has Jerusalem. They're gonna see a guy who's Jewish doing Elvis and it's gonna trigger in their head a whole bunch of stuff about their own Jewish identity. You're doing a holy thing in a holy city.
SCHMELVIS: Alright. But I think you're all full of crap.

(*Schmelvis sings "Simen Tov" and "Mozel Tov." An ISRAELI SOLDIER stands at the edge of the crowd watching, an M-16 rifle slung over his back. Schmelvis convinces him to strum his rifle like a guitar as Schmelvis sings.*)

(*Rabbi Poupko runs into HOWARD WISEBAND, who used to be the director of the Jewish Federation of Memphis in the 60s.*)

RABBI: Tell them the story.
WISEBAND: The story is that Elvis used to come in with his buddies to the Memphis Jewish Community Center to play racquetball after midnight. We'd open the doors for them. When he was young and growing up, his family didn't have much money and the Jewish Community Center gave him a scholarship to the daycare. As a result, he felt very close to the Jewish community.
SCHMELVIS: Did you know he was Jewish?
WISEBAND: That was the word on the street, yeah.

DAY 4

Director's Log, Nov. 3, 2000

We went to the Haddasah Forest to plant a tree for Elvis, the traditional rite to honor dead Jewish ancestors. We got off to a bad start when the Rabbi said to Schmelvis: "I paid $10 for this. Get your own tree. This is for Elvis. If you want to plant a tree for your dead grandmother, go ahead."

But the rabbi calmed down. We planted the tree and Poupko gave a blessing: "We are gathered here this day to plant a tree for a lost son of the Jewish people, Elvis Aaron Presley. All of us have just been witness to history. It's the first time a tree has been planted in the state of Israel for Elvis Aaron Presley. Roots which have been severed have now been reconnected."

Evan and the Rabbi embrace. Then, as Schmelvis sings an impromptu song, everybody starts dancing. Poupko does a bizarre chicken dance.

> We're planting a tree
> For Elvisssss Presssssleeeeee . . .
>
> Oh won't you come with me
> To the land of the holy
>
> We're planting a tree
> Elvisssss Presssssleeeeee . . .
>
> Oh won't you come, come with me
> To the Holy Land

"I think a rabbi prancing and dancing around as we plant a tree for Elvis Presley is the first sign of the apocalypse," said Jonathan as we left.

In the room at night, Ari tells me about how he's going to Paris in a month and how he's going to be staying with his Parisian cousins who love him to death. He says that the second he walks through the door, they're all over him, literally knocking him to the floor and rolling all over him. It sounds like 101 DALMATIANS.

"A-rrri," they yell.

We lie on our cots and Ari tells me all the details, which I love.

"They cook me meals. All this stuff with all these sauces. They stop in the middle while they're cooking and they start dancing. I sit there at the kitchen table and they dance over to me and sit on my lap and dance in my lap."

I can just see Ari sitting there, his eyes darting all over the place, just sitting there, being a nice guy and being appreciated for it. Coming to Paris and reaping all the rewards for being such a nice guy. It must be good to know that there's a place out there where all these girls will pig pile you because they think you're such a nice guy.

Ari writes a poem on a discarded falafel restaurant place mat:

There was a southern
Jew named Elvis
who was just like other people
other people who weren't Jewish
except he wasn't like them.
not really.

He wore his hair funny
and wiggled his hips like a girl
and people thought he was weird
maybe that he was a homo
because he dressed in weird stuff
and loved his mother in a weird sort of way
and he married a girl who was only twelve.

And he had a manager who had an
accent like Henry Kissinger
and man did this man love money
he made Elvis make all these weird films
where he wore cowboy hats and beat up people
but deep down inside, under all the hairspray
and Brut aftershave (Elvis's favorite brand)
there was a little Jew.

A tiny little Jew
whose family came from the schtetl.
Who would have been burnt in the ovens
if he had the misfortune of being born in Europe
instead of America
where he made birthday albums for his mama
because the Nazis would have known.

That's how they did things
they found out who your mama was
and then who her mama was
and who her mama was.

Like they were torah scholars
or genealogists.
Elvis would have been somebody's dead
grandfather who

[the rest of this poem is too smeared in falafel grease and hot sauce to be read]

Director's Log, Nov. 11, 2000 — Research Notes

There are places in Israel where for under $5 you can create your own falafel. There is an entire buffet-style table set up at which you can pack your pita pocket full of various salads, olives, creamy dips, and even french fries. Actual french fries! You can pack that pocket until the point of absurdity, until there's red liquid saturating the bread and hummus is leaking out of holes. Oh ya, in the middle of eating the fat sloppy bastard you can get up and go back to the buffet table and pack it some more! It's gold.

Our Israeli friends are in fact using the falafel pocket not so much as a pita but as some kind of bowl. A bowl that one might continually refill. This whole all-you-can-eat falafel, this continual work-in-rogress, this grotesque, delightful phenomenon is something I can hardly wrap my head around. There are so many questions that still need to be asked, on the level of hygiene, economics. Evan, ever the existentialist, says there are certainly a couple of ontological questions. He says it's a conundrum, a riddle for the ages. And for once I have to agree with him.

Jonathan's Journal

We go to a Bedouin camel camp to take publicity shots of Schmelvis on a camel. It turns out that it isn't so authentic. Instead of Bedouins, it's run by Israelis and the biggest camel is named Ben Gurion. We all get to ride the camels to a tent where we feast as Schmelvis plays guitar and we all join in with impromptu glass percussion playing.

JERUSALEM, BEDOUIN CAMEL CAMP.

Evan and Ari lean back after a big meal and watch the desert.

ARI: That was the best meal so far.
EVAN: And what a view.

I had this image of myself covered in Dead Sea mud, walking around like a zombie, beautifying myself in this sacred soil from head to toe. We couldn't find a stinking ounce. There was one little hole of the stuff, the size of my fist, that two overweight thirteen year-olds had been digging away at for the past three hours. They've only managed to cover one shoulder each. Maybe they're running low on mud. Maybe the Japs have depleted our muddiest natural resource. Foolish human vanity! In the absence of mud, I decide to float.

THE DEAD SEA, THE BEACH.

Evan and Jonathan float in the water.

EVAN: This is so beautiful.
JONATHAN: You know what's beautiful? That topless Swiss woman
cavorting on the rocks over there.
EVAN (*looking into the camera*): This isn't the lowest point on
earth. That (*pointing to Jonathan*) is the lowest point on earth.

(*Suddenly, they are surrounded by THREE CHASSIDIC ORTHODOX JEWS.*)

EVAN: What sect of *Chassidim* are you from?
CHASSID #1 (*pointing up in the air*): From God.
JONATHAN: You know why we came to Israel? To prove that Elvis
Presley is Jewish. Do you think it's a worthwhile thing to do?
CHASSID #1: No.
JONATHAN: What do you think we should spend our time doing?
CHASSID #1: To work and make some money.
JONATHAN: Do you know how much money we spent on this enterprise?
CHASSID #1: How much?
JONATHAN: Silly money. You're going to think we're idiots. I'm
going to spare my own dignity and not tell you.

(*The two other Chassids start to sing in Hebrew. When they finish
singing, Jonathan turns to them.*)

JONATHAN: We found out that Elvis Presley is Jewish. Do you think
that's important or not important?
CHASSID #2: It is.
JONATHAN: How come?
CHASSID: Music turns the world upside down.
JONATHAN: Does the bible talk about the importance of Rock'n'Roll?
CHASSID: It talks about the *nginnah* [music]. Any style of *nginnah*
is important.
EVAN: So the fact that Elvis Presley may be Jewish is one more
step toward bringing on the Messianic Age?
CHASSID: It is.
EVAN: Wow.

In the back of the van riding through the desert coming back from the Dead Sea. Evan and Ari and I were singing an obnoxiously loud and impassioned version of "Lean on Me." After a few minutes, Mila, driving up front, becomes so disgusted he turns on the radio to drown us out. And there was the Hebrew DJ introducing the next song, "Lean on Me."

Schmelvis wouldn't give us the satisfaction of admitting we had just witnessed a miracle. Evan kept saying to him, "You're religious. Aren't you freaked out?" But Schmelvis wouldn't say a thing. We figured he was just jealous that God had reached out to us and not him. Anyway, that kind of serendipity used to be the kind of thing that would have made me happy, but nowadays it feels like shit is just so random that it's absolutely scary sometimes. Just the same, Evan and me high-fived each other all the way back to Jerusalem.

Jonathan's Journal

I still don't know why we came to Israel. We got nothing. It's like we're bringing back a T-shirt that says, "My grandmother went to Israel and all she brought me back was this lousy movie" . . . or rather "Auntie Pearlie's money went to Israel and all she got was heartache."

Director's Log, Nov. 5, 2000 — Research Notes

In the '68 comeback special, Elvis's leather jumpsuit was so tight they had to pull it apart and literally sew it on him.

His death was brought on by anaphylactic shock due to an allergy to codeine. He had dental work done the morning of his death and, though he knew codeine would kill him, he insisted the dentist give him some. He took it before bed, woke up in the night, stumbled to the bathroom and promptly died on the floor. Urban legend says he died on the toilet, which I guess would be more appropriate. However, if that hadn't killed him, he would've died shortly anyway because his liver had literally ceased to function. In fact, the reason for Elvis's bloated appearance toward the end was not his weight, it was that his body was full of toxic fluids.

Elvis saw Jackie Wilson perform in the late 50's and thought he was the second coming. Wilson was known for sweating profusely onstage and this struck Elvis as the mark of a true performer. When he visited Wilson backstage, Wilson shared his secret — right before taking the stage he'd pop salt pills by the dozen and gulp down gallons of water. Elvis made this his m.o., not only to sweat himself up onstage but also to lose weight. Elvis being Elvis, however, he substituted Coke for water. Hence his famously pathetic preference for towering Dixie cups of Coke.

There's a story from the Led Zeppelin biography that is not repeated in any Elvis book I know of. When Led Zeppelin was in Vegas, Elvis sent for Plant and Page. Not surprisingly, they found him doped out of his mind, sullen, silent, surrounded by silent groupies, bottles of Coke, and guns. Plant thought he'd break the ice by doing his Elvis impersonation. He burst into "Treat Me Like a Fool." Elvis fixed him with his bloodshot eyes and stared him down like a prison bitch. Plant sank to the bed and said not another word. There he sat with Page for several hours, while Elvis drank Coke and watched a television that wasn't turned on. Finally, they said their good-byes and went for the door. When they were halfway down the hall, Elvis ran out after them, crooned "Treat me like a fool . . ." just like Plant had sung it, bid them farewell like they were his best friends in the world, then disappeared back into his room.

Elvis's last movie starred him as a martial arts messiah, saving the world with the mystical power of his ka-rah-tay. Though the film went to camera, it was never completed.

The three best-known western names in China: Jesus Christ, Richard Nixon, and Elvis Presley.

Director's Log, Nov. 6, 2000

When we set out on this journey, our intention was to christen Elvis Jewish and bring him to the world. We thought we would be met with some kind of strong sentiment.

e.g. "This is an outrage." "How goddam wonderful. How simply divine and useful."

What we got instead was a lot of people who couldn't care less. People of all walks of life, of all creeds and religions, all of them unanimous in their decision that Elvis's Jewishness could not possibly mean less to their basic enjoyment of life. We even tried egging them on. We made pathetic pleas: "Look at me! Look at me as I speak the truth of Elvis's true religion. Watch me as I set the world on fire, paradoxically before the advent of rock'n'roll, watch me as myself and my merry band of pranksters speak the unbelievable."

But still the same response.

e.g. In Memphis: "Why would that get my goat? Elvis loved all the races of the rainbow."

e.g. In Israel: (Sounds of bombs going off in the not too distant distance.) "Elvis a Jew? So? Good for him."

Have we become so jaded, so full of force-fed books with lists of Famous Jews and *People* magazine Jewish celebrity fun facts and gossipy tidbits that a piece of information like that can only be met with a big fat yawn?

When we set out on these trips, we really thought that people would care. No one cared. Not one person's life was changed. Perhaps that's as it should be.

Possible movie title: "Elvis is Jewish (and nobody cares)."

Director's Log, Nov. 14, 2000

Schmelvis has been calling every day since we returned wanting to know how he is going to be portrayed, threatening me one minute, becoming wistful and nostalgic the next, then threatening again. "I wish we were back in Israel. It was great. Eating falafel in Jerusalem, swimming in the Dead Sea. It was like a fairy tale. The whole experience seemed like movie." I remind him: "It was a movie." He shoots back: "Yeah, let's just hope it's not a bad movie."And then he hangs up abruptly.

Today he called telling us about an Elvis festival in Memphis. There's an Elvis Karaoke Contest and the World's Largest Elvis Impersonator Contest. We decide to return. Everybody except the Rabbi, who Schmelvis insists can't come. And this time we fly. Jonathan refuses ever to set foot in a Winnebago again. Anyway, Ari's still paying off the $1,400 in damages to the Winnebago that was charged to his VISA.

Part 4

MEMPHIS AIRPORT HOLIDAY INN, HALLWAY.

Evan and Max try to convince Schmelvis to participate in an Elvis karaoke contest.

EVAN (*approaching Schmelvis*): I just spoke to the contest organizer. She says it's a real karaoke contest. You can't use your guitar.
SCHMELVIS: Then I'm not going on.
EVAN: You've got to. The whole point of karaoke is to sing along with recorded music.
SCHMELVIS: If I can't go out there with my guitar and one of you Jewboys holding the microphone for me, I'm not going on. That's the bottom line.
EVAN: It's not personal. It's karaoke! That's it. I'm freaking out. I'm leaving.
MAX: Come on, Schmel, we've come 1500 miles for you to crash this karaoke contest. You'll be insulting all these people if you go out there with a guitar. It's like you're saying that karaoke is some kind of cheesy....
SCHMELVIS: It's very cheesy!

(*He walks away. Max follows him.*)

MAX: If you do this, you might have a whole new career in Japan, performing at the Yokohama Holiday Inn in front of thousands of adoring Japanese fans. You'll make a fortune.
EVAN: I can't believe we brought you all this way. Do you know how much money we spent to come here?
SCHMELVIS (*sitting down with his arms folded*): You guys are pathetic, all of you. That's the bottom line.

Pamphlet handed out in the parking lot of the Holiday Inn

Daily Memphis Messiah

Have you accepted Elvis Presley as your personal savior?

For your soul to pass the pearly gates of Graceland, you must repent sinner!
The benevolent King of Rock'n'Roll/Creation hands down the following Ten
Commandments:

1) Thou shalt not step on the Lord's blue suede shoes.
2) Thou shalt honor thy showgirl.
3) Thou shalt wear rhinestone-studded jumpsuits.
4) Thou shalt not covet they neighbor's sideburns.
5) Thou shalt observe the Sabbath . . . except for the albums without
   Ozzy.
6) Thou shalt eat only peanut butter and 'nanna sandwiches.
7) Thou shalt not shoot out the television set.
8) Thou shalt not take drugs, except by prescription.
9) Thou shalt not let thy daughter marry Michael Jackson.
10) Thou shalt not worship any false gods, including Elvis Costello.

Director's Log, Nov. 28, 2000

After the karaoke fiasco, we stumble into a huge ballroom set up for Images of Elvis—the world's largest Elvis impersonator contest. Schmelvis and Evan calmed down and we started to plan how we were going to crash the contest. Schmelvis was very excited about introducing himself to his Elvis impersonator colleagues from around the world. The stage is set up with a huge American flag and Schmelvis is going to go up and pose in front of it à la Patton.

MEMPHIS AIRPORT HOLIDAY INN, BALLROOM.

Nobody is using the stage, so Schmelvis climbs aboard and practices his schtick while Max tries to direct. A WOMAN approaches.

WOMAN: Is he registered in the contest? Registration closes in half an hour.
MAX: You mean he can still get into the contest? I thought it's just the elite impersonators from around the world.
WOMAN: Anybody can register who has $50. Only the best ones get into the finals on Friday night.

(She walks away.)

MAX: I'm registering you. Just think of the platform it would give you to tell the world Elvis was a Jew.
DAN: Not only is he entering the contest, he's going to win. I'm going to coach him. I'm going to be his Colonel Tom.
SCHMELVIS: But the finals are Friday night. It's the Sabbath. I won't be able to perform.
EVAN (*whispering to Max*): If he gets into the finals, I'll eat a yarmulke and walk naked through the Holiday Inn singing "Hava Nagila."

The group walks over with Schmelvis to the registration table.

WOMAN AT TABLE: What's your name?
SCHMELVIS: Schmelvis. S-H-M-E-L-V-I-S.
MAX: No, S-C-H-
SCHMELVIS: OK, S-C-H-
WOMAN: Who are y'all?
DAN: We're doing a documentary. We're from Canada.
WOMAN: Is this a comic act?
MAX: No, it's not a comic act.
WOMAN: Because if this is a comic act, you're not welcome. Is this a comic act, Schmelllvissss? Your costume looks funny.
SCHMELVIS: No, it's serious. I'm a Jewish Elvis impersonator. I would never make fun of Elvis.

MEMPHIS AIRPORT HOLIDAY INN, CONFERENCE ROOM.

The entire crew help Schmelvis prepare for the contest.

DAN: OK, you've got fifteen minutes to perform. That's enough for three songs. What are you going to sing? How about starting off with "Heartbreak Hotel"?
SCHMELVIS: Do you know the words?
DAN: How about "Jailhouse Rock"?
SCHMELVIS: How does it go?
DAN: You were going to do "Suspicious Minds" at the karaoke contest. How about that?
SCHMELVIS: OK, but I only know half the words. The other half I make up.
DAN: What do you know?
SCHMELVIS: "Simen Tov and Mazel Tov."
EVAN: He doesn't know one Elvis song? What have you been doing all these years?

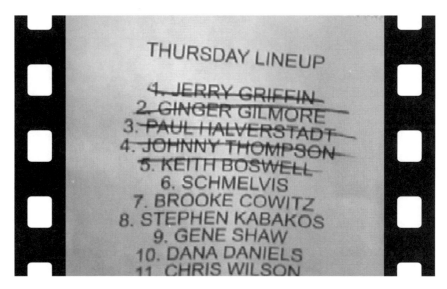

THURSDAY LINEUP
1. JERRY GRIFFIN
2. GINGER GILMORE
3. PAUL HALVERSTADT
4. JOHNNY THOMPSON
5. KEITH BOSWELL
6. SCHMELVIS
7. BROOKE COWITZ
8. STEPHEN KABAKOS
9. GENE SHAW
10. DANA DANIELS
11. CHRIS WILSON

MEMPHIS AIRPORT HOLIDAY INN, BALLROOM.

During sound check, Schmelvis does a dress rehearsal in his white polyester suit. He keeps screwing up, even the lines to "Teddy Bear," and the crew has to correct him over and over. The contest organiser, DOC FRANKLIN, comes in.

DOC FRANKLIN: You're not allowed to change any of the words. You have to sing like Elvis.
MAX: Don't worry.
DOC: We'll be keeping an eye on you.

(He points to a big burly bouncer with the name "Butch" on an ID tag.)

DOC: My son-in-law is a deputy sheriff and he won't tolerate any funny business. I just don't trust you. Your costume is funny-looking. I don't like this. I tell you what. He can go out and do his first song and I'll watch. If it's OK, then you can bring your cameras out and film the rest of his act.
MAX: No problem.
DOC: We ran El Vez outta town and don't think we won't run you out if there's any funny business.

(Doc walks away.)

MAX (*to Schmelvis*): Walk out there, grab the mic, say "Now I'm going to do a tribute to Elvis's spiritual side" and knock out "Amazing Grace" and you'll have them eating out of your hand. Once you got them in your side pocket, that's when you cold-cock them with an uppercut of reality. "Elvis was a Jew," you tell them matter-of-factly. "He was a yid, ladies and gentleman."It'll be like a cross between a smartbomb, an unexpected suppository and a prank call from the elders of Zion. And while they're still clutching at their worry beads, you launch into "Simen Tov, Mazel Tov," saying that Elvis used to sing it at the Memphis Jewish Community Centre as a teenager. This will happen as camera number one zooms in on your face, and camera number two pans the crowd for reactions.
SCHMELVIS: Is that true? Elvis really sang "Simen Tov"?
MAX: How the hell do I know? It's possible.
SCHMELVIS: I don't like this. You heard what they did to El Vez.

BALLROOM, BACKSTAGE.

The crew and Schmelvis wait in the wings. Schmelvis is next. Doc approaches.

DOC: I want you to promise me before you go on. No religion and no politics. (*Schmelvis hesitates*) Why isn't he answering?
MAX: He's confused. He's going to sing "Amazing Grace," that's religious.
DOC: Amazing Grace is OK, but I don't want any religion or politics. Promise me.

(*Schmelvis says nothing.*)

DAN: That's southern hospitality?

184

DOC (*yelling*): I don't give a damn, I'm saying no religion and no politics! I don't want any! Do I make myself clear?

(*A ten-year-old GIRL Elvis impersonator with a pompadour, the act following Schmelvis, watches the scene with her GRANDMOTHER.*)

GRANDMOTHER (*to Schmelvis*): You have to know in your heart what you want to do.
SCHMELVIS (*taking Max aside*):I don't like this. Maybe we should cancel.
MC: Ladies and gentlemen, Schmelvis!

(*The MC comes to the wings and yells.*)

Schmelvis, you're on! (*Schmelvis doesn't move.*)

DOC: Make an announcement. Cancel Schmelvis. The next act is cancelled.
EVAN: Why isn't he going out on stage?
ARI: I don't know.
EVAN: We came here for him to go out on stage. They're announcing Schmelvis and the stage is empty. It doesn't get any more nihilistic than this.

(*On their way out, the ten-year-old girl impersonator prepares to go on.*)

GIRL (*to Schmelvis*): This event is not about politics or religion.

MEMPHIS AIRPORT HOLIDAY INN, HALLWAY.

The gang hails Schmelvis, their conquering hero.

ARI: I'm really proud of Schmelvis. I don't blame him for not wanting to face those redneck bastards.
JONATHAN: Elvis had more of a sense of humor than these people. He said he liked the imitations Andy Kaufman did of him.
DAN: These people are like player pianos, playing the same homage to Elvis over and over. No individuality. Elvis would be disgusted.
ARI: We're proud of you. How you feeling, Schmel?
SCHMELVIS: I wouldn't mind getting out of this suit.
EVAN: I'm not getting any of this. Is it me, or did we just blow the whole thing here?
JONATHAN: We just hit the climax.
EVAN: That wasn't a climax!
JONATHAN: Just sit back and enjoy your dénouement.

Director's Log, Nov. 29, 2000 — Research Notes

I consulted my *Idiot's Guide to Elvis*. It turns out Doc Franklin used to be Elvis's veterinarian. His most famous patient was Scatter, Elvis's scotch-addicted pet chimpanzee, who would join his master for cocktails every afternoon and watch TV. The chimp ended up dying of cirrhosis of the liver.

Now He Is Our Elvis

a poem by Ari Cohen

Now he is our Elvis

Now he is our Elvis
because the other ones are weird
and smell of formaldehyde

he is our pudgy sweet Elvis
cute that he has sardine juice in his beard
because he is ours
and he let us drag him around
and said:
"Step on my blue suede shoes! Why not?
They're only shoes."

MEMPHIS AIRPORT HOLIDAY INN, CONFERENCE ROOM.

*Down the hall from the Elvis impersonator contest, a black
Christian ministry is holding a service. The crew attends.*

BLACK WOMAN PREACHER (*shouting*): The devil cannot hold you down
when God has a grip on your soul!
CONGREGATION: Preach on, sister!
PREACHER: Trust in the Lord! Reach out to him! He's stronger than
Satan!
CONGREGATION: That's right!
PREACHER: Don't be tempted by material things. All you need is
Jesus.
CONGREGATION: Hallelujah!
PREACHER: I notice that some of you here today are with the imper-
sonator contest. (*pointing to Jonathan*) Will the young man sitting
over there please come up and join me?

(*Looking sheepishly, Jonathan walks to the front of the room to
receive the minister's blessing.The preacher and the piano player
join hands with him to form a circle and they pray.*)

The preacher took my hand, closed her eyes and started praying really hard. The whole time this was happening, I was scared that somehow I was going to fall on the floor and start speaking in tongues, maybe even rolling around, rolling right out the door across the hall into the Elvis impersonator contest where Doc and his boys would get on top of me to perform some impromptu logrolling in their cowboy boots.

At the end of the service, the preacher invites Schmelvis to the front of the room to accompany her and the piano player in a rendition of "Amazing Grace."

MAX (to Evan): Talk about redemption. Schmelvis set out to bring Elvis back to Judaism. Now he's finally singing his heart out . . . in a church!

Schmelvis's Amazing Grace

Amazing grace
how sweet
the sound
that saved
a kvetch
like me.

I once
was lost
but now
I'm found
in the sea
of Galilee.

A bitter poem by Ari

DID YOU KNOW ELVIS WAS JEWISH?

Did you know Elvis was Jewish
as the hunchbacked sewermen worry of their hernias?

Did you know Elvis was Jewish
as the newborn weep for loss of the womb?

Did you know Elvis was Jewish
the earth is hurtling through chaos?

Did you know Elvis was Jewish
and my father never realized his dream of walking on the moon?

Elvis was Jewish I promise
and the millions of unloved landladies mourn for dead Graceland.

STREETS OF MEMPHIS

Jonathan and Evan take a ride in a tourist horse and buggy.
Max thought it might make a nice scene, the two childhood friends
riding off into the distance.

JONATHAN: I finally realized what this film is about. It's about
failure. Noble failure. No, it's not even about noble failure.
It's about lazy, pathetic failure.
EVAN: Are you calling Schmelvis, Elvis, and all of us gathered
here lazy, pathetic failures?
JONATHAN: I think there have been some great works of art about
failure. (*pause*) I don't think this is one of them, but there you
go....

FADE OUT

Jonathan's notes towards a novel he will never finish

Elvis's great-great-grandmother on his mother's side was a Jew and a prominent Montreal rabbi thought Elvis's lost Jewish identity could be the perfect metaphor for the plight of the Diaspora Jew in the twentieth century. The Producer hit his rich old aunt up for a lot of money, a director was named and a crew was assembled. Since every film needs a star, a Chassidic Elvis impersonator named Schmelvis was brought on board to perform impromptu Brechtian musical numbers and to generally add some glitz to the project. It was supposed to be his adventure, his spiritual quest. That's what The Director told him and Schmelvis would state it every chance he got. Before we left, a CBC documentary crew came out to see us off and to interview Schmelvis.

"I'm on a spiritual quest," he would eagerly repeat, apropos of nothing.

The CBC left and all seven of us piled into the rented Winnebago, the Winnebagel, joked The Director, and drove for twenty-odd hours straight to Memphis. The Rabbi flew into Memphis and then rented a Cadillac to meet up with us.

The idea was that the film was going to be as much about Elvis the Jew as it was to be about the colorful characters who inhabited the Winnebago.

"This isn't going to work," I said to The Director about an hour into the trip. "No one cares if Elvis is a Jew or not."

"This is great," he said, all excited as he drove along. "We have to save this conversation for the movie."

That's how it was with everything I said.

"Why don't we have a scene," I said, "where you're telling me this would be great for the movie."

"We should," said The Director.

We hadn't even hit the American border and the Winnebago was becoming a postmodern hall of mirrors.

"There has to be a scene where everyone's having fun on the RV," he said into the rear view mirror. "Pass around the football."

Every so often, along the way, The Director would force Schmelvis into his Elvis jumpsuit to sing a song for the locals in front of the camera. Schmelvis would often hide in the Winnebago bathroom, refusing to come out.

"This is why we brought you here," the director would yell. "This is the reason why you're here."

I'm convinced that the best scene of the film will occur at the moment where Schmelvis walks out of the Winnebago, in a crowded Piggly Wiggly parking lot, all decked out in his Star of David red cape, and stands in the doorway for a moment, just looking at us.

"You're all pathetic," he says with a look of pure disgust.

Before the movie, Schmelvis's only gigs were at religious parties and old age homes. He would come out in his jumpsuit and Elvis sunglasses and sing "Hava Nagila." The Director met Schmelvis one day while visiting his grandmother at the nursing home. He was performing in the solarium and the director's grandmother liked him very much. Schmelvis was convinced that the film was going to make his career.

The first thing we did when we got down South was set off to find the grave of Nancy Burdine, Elvis's great-great-grandmother, to see if there was a Jewish star on it. After stopping in every cemetery we could find along the road, The Rabbi finally lost it.

"This isn't how you do research," The Rabbi said. "Research means sitting in a library. You open a book. You look through archives. You visit a city hall. This is how children do research!"

The Rabbi, of course, was right. But we still had an RV full of colorful characters.

The Rabbi and Schmelvis did not get along. It had to do with the fact that Schmelvis was a proselytizer and The Rabbi wasn't. If you were to look at our group in the way one would look at the cast of characters in a Restoration play, you would place The Rabbi at the top of the hierarchy while The Schmelvis would go at the very bottom. When The Rabbi would lay it into him, Schmelvis would say things that didn't make sense.

"That's an acute observation," he would say.

The Rabbi referred to being around Schmelvis as suddenly being surrounded by a cocoon of idiocy; but sometimes, like the holy fool of the *Shtetl*, Schmelvis would inadvertently come out with statements of definite wisdom and beauty.

Schmelvis and The Rabbi finally bonded in what I think will be one of the highlights of the film. Sitting in the bar at the Peabody Hotel, they both tag-teamed me, accusing me of being a self-hating Jew because I questioned the relevance of Elvis's Jewishness.

"Never mind if Elvis is a Jew," yelled Schmelvis, pointing his finger into my face, "are you a Jew?"

The Rabbi liked that one. They went at me for a good fifteen minutes accusing me of every sin you could think of. The Director sat off to the side having to almost hold his groin to keep from peeing himself for joy.

On the final day we went to Graceland so that The Rabbi could say *kaddish*, the Jewish prayer for the dead, over Elvis's grave. We wanted to get together a ten-man *minyan*, but we eventually settled on seven.

After The Rabbi said *kaddish*, he got into his Cadillac and we got back into the Winnebago.

Schmelvis and I sat at the kitchen table. As the RV pulled out, we pressed the bottoms of our beer cans hard against the table.

"You know," said Schmelvis, "I don't even care if Elvis is Jewish or not."

"What about your spiritual quest?" I asked.

"Elvis was a loser," he said. "He never knew who he was. He died on a toilet. He's dead now, God rest his soul."

Schmelvis put on his Elvis sunglasses and took a pull from his beer.

The RV toilet stank like hell and I wasn't the type to pee out the window. I crossed my legs real tight.

"Stop the winnebago," I yelled up front. "Stop the goddamn winnebago!"

Appendix

Who's Who of Famous Jews

Abdul, Paula—Singer

Aldrin, Buzz—Second astronaut to walk on the moon

Allen, Woody—Comedian, actor, director, producer

Alpert, Herb—Leader, Tijuana Brass

Bacall, Lauren—Actress

Beastie Boys—Hip hop group (all of them)

Beck—Musician

Berlin, Irving—Composer of the song "White Christmas"

Biafra, Jello—Singer, American punk band Dead Kennedys

Bialik, Mayim—Actress, TV show "Blossom"

Bolan, Marc—Member of rock group T. Rex

Borgnine, Ernest—Actor

Brooks, Albert—Actor, director

Brooks, Mel—Actor, director, comedian, writer

Bullock, Sandra—Actress

Carew, Rod—Baseball superstar (convert)

Carter, Nell—Actress (convert)

Cass, "Mama"—Actress

Chomsky, Noam—American philosopher

Cohen, Leonard—Songwriter

Cosell, Howard—Sports broadcaster

Crawford, Joan—Actress

Crystal, Billy—Actor, comedian

Curtis, Tony—Actor

Davis, Jr., Sammy—Singer, actor, dancer (convert)

DeNiro, Robert—Actor (Jewish mother)

Dreyfuss, Richard—Actor

Duchovny, David—Actor, "The X-Files"

Dylan, Bob—Musician

Eisner, Michael—Head of Disney

Escher, M.C.—Artist, explorer of the infinite

Farrell, Perry—Rock musician, founder of Lollapalooza festival

Ford, Harrison—Actor (Jewish mother)

Garfunkel, Art—Singer

Gellar, Sarah Michelle—Actress, "Buffy the Vampire Slayer"

Gershwin, George—Composer, "Rhapsody in Blue"

Ginsberg, Allen—Poet

Goldblum, Jeff—Actor

Gere, Richard—Actor

Gifford, Kathie Lee Epstein—Talk show hostess (converted to Christianity)

Grant, Cary—Actor

Greenberg, Hank—Hall of Fame baseball star

Grodin, Charles—Actor

Guthrie, Arlo—Singer (Jewish mother)

Hepburn, Audrey—Actress

Hamlisch, Marvin—Composer

Hoffmann, Abbie—Political activist

Hoskins, Bob—Actor

Iggy Pop—Musician

Jeremy, Ron—Porn star

Joel, Billy—Musician

Jolson, Al—Singer, mummer, cantor

Keitel, Harvey—Actor

King, Carol—Songwriter/singer

Knopfler, Mark—Musician, Dire Straits

Kravitz, Lenny—Musician

Kissinger, Henry—Former U.S. Secretary of State

Klein, Calvin—Fashion designer

Knopfler, Mark—Rock musician

Koufax, Sandy—Superstar baseball pitcher (refused to pitch on Saturdays)

Koppel, Ted—Anchor, "ABC Nightline"

Kudrow, Lisa—Actress, "Friends"

Landers, Anne—Advice columnist

Landon, Michael—Actor

Lauren, Ralph—Fashion designer

Lewis, Jerry—Comedian

Lewis, Shari—Puppeteer

Loeb, Lisa—Singer

Louis-Dreyfuss, Julia—Actress, "Seinfeld"

Louise, Tina—Actress, "Gilligan's Island"

Mann, Manfred—Musician

Manson, Marilyn—Rock musician

Margulies, Julieanna—Actress, "ER"

Marley, Bob—Reggae artist (Jewish father, black mother)

Marx, Chico—Comedian

Marx, Groucho—Comedian

Marx, Harpo—Comedian

Monroe, Marilyn — Actress (converted before marrying Arthur Miller)

Moranis, Rick—Actor

Neuwirth, Bebe—Actress, "Cheers"

Newman, Paul—Actor (Jewish mother)

Newman, Randy—Composer, Singer

Newton-John, Olivia—Australian pop singer

Nimoy, Leonard—Actor, "Star Trek"

Patinkin, Mandy—Actor

Peck, Gregory—Actor

Perlman, Itzhak — World — renowned violinist
Peter & Mary — Peter Yarrow & Mary Travers of folk group Peter, Paul and Mary
Phish — Rock group
Raphael, Sally-Jessy — Talk show host
Raffi — Children's entertainer
Ramone, Joey — Punk rocker
Reed, Lou — Singer
Reiser, Paul — Actor, "Mad About You"
Richards, Michael — Actor, "Seinfeld"
Rivera, Geraldo — Talk show host
Roth, David Lee — Van Halen rocker
Ryder, Winona — Actress
Savalas, Telly — Actor
Sandler, Adam — Comedian
Schlessinger, Dr. Laura — Radio therapist
Seagal, Steven — Action movie star
Seinfeld, Jerry — Comedian
Seymour, Jane — Actress (Jewish father)
Shaffer, Paul — David Letterman's sidekick
Shatner, William — Actor, "Star Trek"
Simmons, Gene — Lead singer, Kiss
Simmons, Richard — Exercise guru
Silverstone, Alicia — Actress
Simon, Paul — Musician
Simon, Neil — Playwright
Slash — Guitarist of Guns and Roses
Sondheim, Stephen — Broadway lyricist/composer
Spacek, Sissy — Actress
Spielberg, StevenvDirector
Spitz, Mark — Olympic swimming champion
Springsteen, Bruce — ("He's not Jewish but my mother thinks he is," sings
    Adam Sandler in "The Hanukkah Song")
Spungen, Nancy — Girlfriend of Sex Pistols bassist Sid Vicious
Starr, Ringo — Beatle
Steely Dan — Rock group (Donald Fagen and Walter Becker)
Steinman, Jim — Composer for Meat Loaf, Bonnie Tyler, Céline Dion
Stern, Howard — Radio personality
Stewart, Jon — Comedian
Streisand, Barbra — Singer, actress
Taylor, Elizabeth — Actress (convert)
Ustinov, Peter — Actor
Vedder, Eddie — Rock musician, Pearl Jam
Williams, Robin — Comedian, Actor
Winters, Shelley — Actress

Sources: www.yahoodi.com and www.jewhoo.com